HELEN HUGHES 1935

THE MEDIUMSHIP OF HELEN HUGHES

BY
BERNARD UPTON

"Death is the opening of a door where all life is. Man is rising to a consciousness where he is beginning to realise that he is something apart from the body through which he functions."
WHITE FEATHER

First Edition 1946
This Edition 2006

Published by
SDU PUBLICATIONS
www.sdu3.com
ISBN 1-905961-02-2
ISBN 978-1-905961-02-3

Printed and bound by CPI Antony Rowe, Eastbourne

PREFACE TO THIS EDITION

SDU Publications' aim is to reprint books by and about some of the outstanding mediums who demonstrated their abilities during the period 1848 to 1948, the first century of Modern Spiritualism and thereby keep their names alive. All profit from the sale of books is used to re-print another title.

Helen Hughes was a Minister of the Spiritualists' National Union and any list of 'outstanding mediums 1848 to 1948' must include her. To that end I have reprinted this book by Bernard Upton (no relation).

The original book contained no pictures and I am indebted to Psychic Press for allowing me access to their archives. All of the pictures except for the final one are from Psychic Press.

This is our third book in The Pioneer Series, for a list of available titles see end page or visit www.sdu3.com

MINISTER STEVEN UPTON
MAY 2006

CONTENTS

		Page
	Preface To This Edition	4
I	"Miracles" - Ancient And Modern	6
II	Because Of A "Spook"	23
III	The Road-Mender Who Knew	33
IV	Praise From The Press	44
V	"Speaking In Tongues"	57
VI	Astounding Proofs In Public	71
VII	The Trap That Failed	79
VIII	One Of "The Few" Returns	86
IX	The "Mystery Man" Was Convinced	98
X	Striking Testimony	119

CHAPTER I
"MIRACLES" - ANCIENT AND MODERN

Soames (whispering).	Is she inspired?
The Bishop.	Marvellous. Hush....
Soames.	My lord: is this possession by the devil?
The Bishop.	Or the ecstasy of a saint?
Hotchkiss.	Or the convulsion of the pythoness on the tripod?*
The Bishop.	May not the three be one? ...
Mrs. George.	I am a woman: a human creature like yourselves. Will you not take me as I am?
Soames.	Yes; but shall we take you and burn you?
The Bishop.	Or take you and canonise you?

Bernard Shaw, "Getting Married."

A sprightly, rather frail little woman steps upon the platform. Among the thousands waiting to hear her there is a hush of expectancy. Smiling, serene, confident, she faces her audience with an engaging air of friendliness, and with something in her manner implicit of promise. "I shall not disappoint you," she seems to say, "I shall astonish you, inspire you, comfort you. Above all, I shall convince you that this is not an eerie and mysterious subject, but a cheering and enlightening one . . ."

Then follows a remarkable demonstration of that ancient and modern miracle, mediumship - ancient because it is as old as man, modern in the sense that only now is it beginning to be understood. In message after message, delivered with surprising speed and accuracy, she quotes names and addresses, times, places, dates, family relationships and circumstances, the context of conversations, and a hundred-and-one other facts concerning both the living and the dead.

---

*This refers to the Grecian Delphic Oracle. There were many Oracles - really centres of Spiritualism and mediumship. The reputation on of the Oracle at Delphi was partly due to the superiority of the Failing mediums, who were women called Pythonesses

She describes people who have died, but who, to her, are still living on another plane of existence. She reveals intimate details known only to the recipients - and sometimes facts which even they do not know, but which are subsequently verified. She is almost invariably correct, and the spectators, whatever their predilections, listen startled, mystified, marvelling and admiring. It is safe to say that the scorn of even the severest sceptics is shaken before the end of the meeting.

Those who know her will have had little difficulty in recognising this description of Mrs. Helen Hughes, one of the best-known and most admired mediums in Great Britain. She is more than merely popular - she is genuinely loved by her audiences, and has thousands of friends, known and unknown, all over the country. To quote "Psychic News": "She is one of the most beloved mediums that Spiritualism has ever produced and has been dubbed 'Helen the well-beloved.' Everywhere she goes, people stop her in the streets to thank her for the consolation her mediumship has brought them."

This reputation was not easily won, and is not ephemeral. It is founded both upon the high quality of her mediumship and the generous use she makes of it. She excels in matter and in manner, and is as highly developed spiritually as mediumistically.

If Spiritualists are prone to speak in superlatives of her psychic powers, they praise her also for her charming simplicity, allied to that crowning virtue, modesty. She is natural, unassuming, amiable, sincere and utterly unspoiled by success.

What appeals to her audiences most is her wholehearted enthusiasm and cheerful aspect. Her face lights up with pleasure or with warm sympathy as she delivers her messages. She is never enigmatic or obscure, but radiantly earnest, homely and direct.

It is difficult to realise, when one sees her engaged in what is, in effect, a mission of mercy, that many ignorant people condemn it, unseen, as "dealing with the Devil' - as if only that misguided individual were capable of communicating through mediums! That is giving him rather more than his due.

Readers who do not know her may not accept documentary evidence as proof of her powers. Most phenomena, to most people, require to be seen to be believed. I advise such sceptics to test the facts for themselves.

The purpose of this book is to present a record of the evidence for the survival of the human personality provided by this remarkable medium alone. The mass of evidence secured through other mediums is overwhelming. As Sir William Crookes, F.R.S., the great British scientist, wrote in "Phenomena of Spiritualism," "To reject the recorded evidence on this subject is to reject all human testimony whatever, for no fact in sacred or profane history is supported by a stronger array of proofs."

Helen Hughes, certainly added to that array. I have good reasons for believing in Spiritualism. There is no other subject which concerns humanity more vitally, yet about which it knows less. I believe from personal experience and study that our survival of that apparently complete catastrophe, that utter dissolution, known as death, has been proved, and that communication with the so-called dead is an everyday event. Among those who have afforded me the proof, I number Mrs. Helen Hughes.

As a journalist I have never written with greater conviction, nor, I trust, with greater justification, than now. I should not have undertaken this task without believing in its implications, and I am prepared to testify to the truth. "Here I stand; and I can do no other."

There are three schools of thought regarding psychic phenomena - (1) those who do not believe that psychic phenomena take place at all; (2) those who admit that psychic phenomena occur, but who deny that they are "extra-terrestrial," or prove Survival; and (3) those who have experience of psychic phenomena, and who believe that they prove communication with "discarnate intelligences" (i.e., other human beings who have died), and, therefore, survival after death.

If the reader accepts this book as an authentic record of the mediumship of Helen Hughes, and does not insist on the untenable hypothesis of fraud, he is faced with these simple alternatives:- (a) that she possesses supernormal powers of mind which enable her to read the past, present and future to an astonishing degree; or (b) that she is directed by intelligent entities on another plane or "vibration" of existence.

Spiritualists believe the last explanation to be the only one which accounts for all the facts.

It is a scientific fact that the visible universe is not the only aspect of matter or of mind. Scientists of late have been delving more and more deeply into the realms of the invisible. Truth has no finality; it is not fixed, but is an expanding quantity. Why do men allow their minds to become rigid and unreceptive, and lose their capacity for wonder and speculation? In an unfolding universe, the mind of man must also unfold. The desire for knowledge is the divinest form of discontent.

The curious and inquiring mind admits no culminating point. Nothing must be rejected as impossible without inquiry. The corridors of time have echoed to the cachinnation of fools crying "impossible" to every discovery they were incapable of understanding. Say, if you wish, "I do not know," "I do not understand," or "I do not believe" - but never, "It is impossible." Psychic phenomena can no more be denied than thunder and lightning.

Spiritualists are not the cranks and simpletons they are depicted to be. The number of intellectual and well-educated people in their ranks grows daily. The callow comments of some of their more ignorant critics are an affront. Though, for the most part, the public are uncritical or, at the least, apathetic, towards new discoveries, they display towards Spiritualism an irrational and sometimes violent hostility. In no other direction is the conglomeration of prejudices, which serve so many people for ideas, more vigorously exercised.

There are many forms of psychic phenomena and many forms of mediumship, all of which throw light upon the profoundest problem of this or any other age - Do the dead survive and can we communicate with them?

The phenomena fall into two classifications - physical and mental. Mental phenomena are sensed by the medium alone, and include clairvoyance, clairaudience, trance, psychometry, inspirational writing, automatic writing, etc.

Physical phenomena produce results having direct appeal to the physical senses of other observers. They include materialisation, transfiguration, direct voice, the production of writing, paintings and photographs without physical contact, telekinesis (movement of objects without visible contact), raps, levitation and apports (the, passing of solid matter through solid matter).

Helen Hughes's mediumship belongs to the mental category.

Although sitters receive what may be termed *secondary* evidence, it is of a highly convincing nature. She is a clairvoyant, a clairaudient, and a trance-control medium.

Clairvoyance means "clear-seeing," and has been defined as "a supernormal mode of perception which results in a visual image being presented to the conscious mind." The medium, in fact, is able to "discern spirits," and to describe them in detail. Clairaudience means "clear-hearing," is similar in operation to clairvoyance, and implies the hearing of spirit voices by supernormal means. When these two gifts are combined in one medium - as with Helen Hughes - the results are remarkable.

Helen Hughes makes greater use of clairaudience than clairvoyance. Although she sees the spirit communicators perfectly, it is quicker and more convincing for her to repeat what they say than to describe their appearance.

Trance has been defined as "a temporary suspension of sensation or volition," and "a state in which the soul seems to have passed out of the body into another stage of being." While in trance the medium may be "controlled" by her guides and other spirit entities, who speak through her. Mrs. Hughes has spoken in trance for fifteen minutes in fluent French and in other languages of which normally she knows scarcely a word.

Whether or not sitters accept these phenomena as proof that the spirits of the dead are really present, they are bound to admit the accuracy of the information the medium imparts.

Uninformed sceptics wildly attempt to explain the evidence away by attributing the validity of her messages to "telepathy" or "thought-reading," which is plausible up to a point, but which falls to the ground when sitters receive correct information on matters of which they know nothing. But since telepathy and thought-reading themselves are probably psychic phenomena, the "explanation" is merely an evasion, and leaves the sceptics in an even deeper difficulty.

The scientific sceptic argues that such demonstrations are not necessarily proof of control by "discarnate intelligences," but only that the medium utilises "paranormal powers" or "extrasensory perception."

These "definitions," though comfortably technical and evasive, are really only alternative terms, and do not explain the phenomena. Spiritualists, however, prefer the term "supernormal" to "supernatural," because they believe all phenomena occur in accordance with natural laws, not yet fully understood.

Scientists who attempt - unsuccessfully - to negative the discoveries of Spiritualism do not realise that all phenomena must accord with known or unknown laws, otherwise they could not occur. Therefore it should be the object of science to discover what these laws are. Sir Oliver Lodge once wrote: "The existence of a spiritual world will have to be recognised not as a matter of faith, but as a branch of the organised system of knowledge that we call science."

To the scientifically-minded Spiritualist, modern knowledge of the atomic structure of matter makes existence on another plane of "vibration" credible and psychic phenomena explicable. Spiritualism, certainly, is not a pure science - but it may become one. Spiritualism *does* produce evidence, and the only logical course is to continue investigating.

As for that inevitable query, "What use is it?" one could write a book in reply. But of what use are books and evidence which people disregard? One might ask: "What use is life?" Whether we know or not, the fact remains that life exists, and so we study it. Psychic phenomena exist, and so we study them to discover what they are.

Briefly, the use of Spiritualism is to prove that life is worth living, and worth living well - because it is the foundation of a vaster future. "The object of science," says Tolstoy, "is to show how people ought to live." Spiritualism has the same object.

Open-minded inquirers, approaching a new subject, concede some value to the opinions of its qualified exponents, and are willing to investigate the facts themselves. Biased persons, on the other hand, neither accept the evidence of others nor dare to test that of their own senses. This is sheer cowardice, and debars them even from the right to debate. Said Mr. J. W. Herries, the well known Scots journalist at an Edinburgh meeting, "It is no longer the mark of the superior person to scoff, but rather the mark of the bigot and ignoramus."

Spiritualists do not, of course, regard those who know nothing of the subject, or who disagree with them, as bigots. The bigots are those who vilify without knowledge or inquiry.

It is not without reason that Spiritualists consider Mrs. Hughes a brilliant medium. She has earned this reputation because her demonstrations are strikingly evidential. She surprises even the most experienced sitters. At every meeting she strikes a new note of drama by transmuting "impossibilities" into facts. I have seen many a priest in the pulpit, and many a speaker of prouder pretensions, do less to prove Survival in an hour's empty oration than I have seen Helen Hughes do in five minutes. Women have been canonised - or burned - for less!

Incidentally, to dispose of one popular fallacy, neither Helen Hughes nor any other medium ever "calls up" or invokes the spirits of the dead. They come of their own accord, and are just as anxious to communicate with us as we are with them. Furthermore, when a medium is in trance, the phenomena are produced *through* her, not *by* her. She plays a completely passive part.

It is one of the penalties of fame - if the term may be applied to mediums - that those who have scaled the heights are expected continually to scale them again. From those to whom much is given, much is required.

Nevertheless, Helen Hughes invariably "electrifies" all her audiences, carrying them with her on a wave-crest of breathless enthusiasm. They share her triumphs by breaking into spontaneous applause. When, very rarely, a message appears to go astray, the memory of the sitter usually proves to be at fault, or the wrong person has attempted to reply. But Helen Hughes is never perturbed.

Deftly and unerringly she unravels the temporary tangle and continues her demonstration.

She is justly famous as a medium. That her fame is limited to the confines where mediumship is understood is the fault of a world which denies recognition to the study of humanity's most momentous problem and prestige to those who alone are able to throw light upon it.

Spiritualism is not only denied fair publicity, but suffers from an excess of adverse publicity, warped by popular prejudice. Lies and calumnies can always be met - even through the restricted publicity at the disposal of Spiritualism - but apathy is difficult to counteract.

Not that good mediums depend on outside publicity. Their gifts speak for themselves, and they have more work than they can cope with. The public, unknowingly, suffer in having the truth kept from them, and because fewer mediums are developed and encouraged to come forward.

The demand for good mediums far exceeds the supply, and most of them are seriously overworked. How strange it is that while this great world spins for ever down the ringing grooves of change, psychic science - the science of the soul - remains neglected and misrepresented.

Indifference is not the only affliction mediums endure. Helen Hughes and her fellow mediums have probably done more to rob death of its terror and tragedy than whole galaxies of theologians, yet despite this - or perhaps because of it! - instead of being honoured and extolled, they dwell under the constant threat of persecution.

Whatever religious freedom has been conferred on the liberated countries of Europe, complete religious - or even philosophical - freedom does not exist in Britain today.

It is neither necessary nor practicable within the scope of this book to survey the present application of the law to Spiritualism. The question is fully explored in standard works, notably two informative and revealing books by Maurice Barbanell, "Rogues and Vagabonds," and "The

Case of Helen Duncan." These grapple trenchantly with those hoary anachronisms, the Vagrancy Act of 1824 and the Witchcraft Act of 1735, under which genuine and gifted mediums are prosecuted, automatically condemned, and imprisoned.

Mediums are not allowed to substantiate their claims in court, nor does the testimony of any number of prominent and reputable Spiritualists as to their genuineness apparently weigh one iota in the scales of justice.

One day, perhaps, the law will discover that science has advanced since 1735, and modern legislation will be framed, capable of dealing with fraud, yet not calculated to convict genuine mediums as a matter of course.

Not only mediums but their adherents can be prosecuted under the iniquitous Witchcraft Act. The "Two Worlds" of February 16, 1945, pointed out, "The charge is one that can be brought and maintained against any person or persons who are parties to holding out any medium as being a genuine medium." How bitterly earnest inquirers into Spiritualism resent this enormity may be imagined.

The law makes no distinction between genuine mediums and charlatans, and implies that all mediumship is a pretence. Of all the religions which flourish in this land - where even heathens may worship idols if they wish - Spiritualism is the only one subject to persecution, the only one which it is neither legal to practise nor profess.

This ludicrous situation obtains notwithstanding the researches of famous scientists and many other unimpeachable investigators over a period of nearly a hundred years. Their books crowd the shelves of libraries throughout the land, but so far as the law is concerned, they might never have been printed. The law, in fact, is an early eighteenth-century ass, standing stock-still in the path of progress. It countenances the anomaly that mediums may be tried, but may not demonstrate the truth. The truth transcends the law!

Are we still emerging from the Dark Ages? The Church, founded on psychic phenomena in the past, stubbornly denies their existence in the present. Yet so-called "miracles" happen every day, all over the world, quite as remarkable as those of biblical times - though they tend not to justify dogmas but the simple fact of Survival. These tremendous events in our midst are foredoomed to obscurity - deliberately shrouded and distorted by superstition.

Spiritualists - contrary to popular belief - make no mystery of their activities. It is their opponents jealous of power and privilege - who create the atmosphere of secrecy, whereby Spiritualism is so grievously maligned. Genuine Spiritualists welcome investigation, and are always willing to fight in the open.

In particular, it is they, above all others, who desire to detect and expose fraud, and to be consulted, as experts should be, as to what is fraudulent. Trickery is rare, and it is grossly unfair and illogical to deride Spiritualism, as so many people do, whenever a fraud is detected. If every profession were damned on account of its frauds, who would escape whipping?

Doubt and distrust are fostered by those who deny Spiritualism a fair hearing. The attitude of all active Spiritualists is: "You are welcome to investigate - but if you do not investigate you are not entitled to condemn." Most of their opponents dare not investigate - they fear the truth too much. The reluctance of the orthodox to examine the facts of psychic phenomena seem to me to prove only one thing - that *they do not believe in what they profess*; for Spiritualism confirms the fundamental belief of all religions, life after death. Most religions, indeed, appear to have degenerated into an irrational form of materialism - a convenient refuge from practical responsibility, a stereotyped substitute for original thinking.

Critics who allege elaborate collusion - a mathematical and physical impossibility in the case of Mrs. Hughes - can produce no evidence in support of their accusation. Quite 99 percent of her messages are accepted as correct. The remaining one percent of doubtful points is due almost entirely to lapses on the part of sitters. To conduct a fraud on the scale suggested, among huge audiences, would involve a prodigious memory, and would be more marvellous than the genuine feat of mediumship itself.

The commonest disparagement of mediumship is: "It is all done in the dark," implying that all phenomena are produced by ingenious conjuring tricks. This is quite untrue. In only a small percentage of phenomena, notably materialisation and direct voice, is darkness or subdued light necessary, because ectoplasm - a substance drawn from the medium and sometimes from the sitters - is extremely sensitive to light. A simple analogy is that of a photographic plate or film. All Helen Hughes's demonstrations take place in full light.

Another hackneyed question - a very unthinking one - is, "Why do mediums accept money if they are genuine?" One might well ask the same question regarding the huge stipends of some eminent ecclesiastics, or regarding the salaries of any professional men and women. They accept money primarily in order to live. Some people apparently imagine that mediums, having relinquished their normal means of livelihood for a more important but usually less lucrative one, should be allowed to starve.

If they did not earn money, most of them would soon be "without visible means of subsistence," and in danger of having to continue their work, not here but on the Other Side!

Nevertheless, many well-known mediums - sacrificing time, toil and trouble - work without accepting a penny in return. With few exceptions those who accept fees have no other source of income. "The labourer is worthy of his hire," and it is no more reasonable to criticise mediums for earning an honest living than, say, doctors or parsons. Their fees are by no means princely, and, far from not deserving remuneration, they would not be overpaid if they were ten times recompensed for their unique services to humankind.

Helen Hughes, in common with many other mediums, has known adversity, sickness and distress. Even now, she is only moderately comfortable, yet her work is beyond the worth of rubies.

She is conspicuous among platform demonstrators because of her clarity, speed and precision, and the variety and validity of the facts she imparts. Her cheerfulness, too, is a tonic to the beholder. A friend once declared that she deserved greater fame than Helen of Troy, and should be known as "Helen of Joy."

Of the first Helen, the poet asked, "Is this the face that launched a thousand ships?" - which, for Helen Hughes, might be paraphrased: "Is this the face that healed a thousand hearts?" Another friend, succumbing to a somewhat obvious pun, called her "the happy medium." Some think of her as the Lady with the Lamp of Knowledge - the Florence Nightingale of Spiritualism - and others as Spiritualism's Joan of Arc.

Strangers sometimes ask ingenuously: "How does she do it? How can you explain it?" The answer to the first question is that she does not "do" it herself, but that, in a sense, it is done for her by visitants from other planes; what she does is to lend herself to the transmission of messages which bridge that not impassable gulf between us and them.

As to how it can be "explained," the question is still being elucidated. All through history, questing and adventurous minds have pressed upon the frontiers of knowledge, and discovery has transported them beyond the bounds of vocabulary. Most things can be "explained" only in terms of their relationship to something else which is known. As we find new worlds to conquer, we need new words to describe them. The unknown is the untranslatable. Psychic phenomena are explicable only in terms of themselves, or are at the most referable to the operation of unknown natural laws. The irrefragable fact is that these phenomena *do* take place. It is their *interpretation* which concerns us most.

Spiritualism - which is really a form of Rationalism, since it embraces all human knowledge - is one of the few religions or forms of inquiry which are obtaining evidence of Survival. Most others content themselves with fruitless reiteration of long discredited dogmas. It is wrong to regard Spiritualism as "only another religion." To some it is a science or philosophy, both ethical and evidential. It is no more beneath the notice of the intellectual Rationalist than of the religionist. It is essentially practical and exploratory, and it can meet and vanquish every challenge.

To quote Professor J. H. Hyslop, Professor of Logic and Ethics at Columbia University: "I regard the existence of discarnate spirits as scientifically proved, and I no longer refer to the sceptic as having any right to speak on the subject. Any man who does not accept the existence of discarnate spirits and the proof of it, is either ignorant or a moral coward. I give him short shrift, and do not propose any longer to argue with him on the supposition that he knows anything about the subject." ("Life After Death.")

If the high priests of mystery have nothing to tell us of continuous revelation, Spiritualism has. It is ushering in a new reformation, another renaissance. The knot it is unravelling by the road is "the knot of human death and fate."

I am grateful to Helen Hughes and other mediums for having convinced me of Survival, and I am glad to have become both her biographer and her friend. I have made many friends because of my interest in Spiritualism. I hope I shall lose none for the same reason, conscious though I am of the persistence of the legend that all those connected with it would be "far better off in a home." Apart from this inept insinuation - which a keen sense of humour, and the company, in this country alone, of hundreds of thousands of other lunatics at large, enable me to view with equanimity - I feel free to tell "the truth, the whole truth, and nothing but the truth," as I see it.

I wrote this book in my spare time while serving in the Army - a task fraught with difficulties. Three years ago I was an agnostic, convinced - as I still am - that, in a sense, all thinking should be scientific, and long-since persuaded of the barrenness of orthodox theology.

I quoted as the crystallisation of my philosophy of life: "I believe only in that which can be demonstrated." Today, like other journalists who have encountered the astonishing facts, I have become a Spiritualist, but I have not had to relinquish that reasonable tenet. I still believe *only in that which can be demonstrated* ... and I believe that Survival and communication with other planes of existence have been and are being demonstrated.

As a newspaper-man, I believe that if psychic phenomena were viewed in their true perspective, much of what the Press ignores today would become "front-page news." Theology seldom made good "copy," but Spiritualism is the story of the century. At all events, it seems to me the most *interesting* of subjects truth always is interesting, because it so seldom sees the light of day! Spiritualism establishes religion, or humanism, on an intellectual and logical basis.

I have attended many séances, lectures and demonstrations, and studied and debated "about it and about" - and I have emerged by a very different door from that through which I entered. I have even ... but that's another story.

I was compelled to re-orientate my materialistic philosophy of life, not through having become credulous, but through having been sedulous. Confronted by the *facts* of psychic phenomena, I had to admit myself wrong - as I always shall if I can add to my knowledge thereby. What is, I believe, the most tremendous truth of all time, was withheld from me too long as it is from millions of others - by the world conspiracy of silence.

Having seen what I have, I should be lacking in intelligence if I did not believe it, and in courage if I did not declare it. My only appeal to the honest sceptic is: "Do not decry: investigate." In the words of Lawrence of Arabia: "Your reward will be in proportion to your effort."

This book cannot be considered a complete "life" of Helen Hughes, since she still has, I hope, many years of valuable work before her. From a mass of material, I have selected some of the highlights of an eventful career, well worthy of delineation.

As it happened, I was assisted in gathering material from her by the period of rest ordered by her medical advisers in February, 1945, because of the threat of acute laryngitis.

This setback was caused by overwork and the discomforts and difficulties of wartime travelling. Reluctant to disappoint her audiences, she fought against the disability until the last moment. One may liken that interval of rest to a milestone in her life. Starting at the outset of her career, I shall make that milestone my destination, and, having reached it, wish her God-speed along the remainder of the road. *Monkseaton, February, 1946.*

HELEN HUGHES

CHAPTER II
BECAUSE OF A "SPOOK"

> "But trailing clouds of glory do we come
> From God who is our home:
> Heaven lies about us in our infancy."
> Wordsworth, "Ode on Intimations of Immortality."

Whatever else sceptics may deny, some facts concerning the early life of Helen Hughes are indisputable, and constitute common ground.

The foreigner who, in filling up a form, replied "Yes" to the terse inquiry: Born - was nothing if not self-evident. That Helen Hughes was born on April 11, 1893, at 64, Adolphus Street, Seaham Harbour, County Durham, the first child of Henry and Margaret Shepherd, is an uncontested fact. That she was a born medium did not become obvious, even to her, for many years. Mediums, like poets, are born not made, but their gifts require recognition and development to become effective. Helen Hughes was destined to tread the pathway to mediumship with slow and painful steps.

The great gift of mediumship sometimes comes to the most obscure. Helen Hughes was born of a humble family, but if spiritual qualities are the true measure of attainment she was richly endowed.

Her father was a bottle-finisher at the Candlish Glass Works, Seaham Harbour, and, since there were seven children - three sons and four daughters - existence was always a problem.

The belief that psychic faculties are hereditary is borne out in her case. Her grandmother on her father's side, Mrs. Jane Shepherd, was strongly mediumistic. From the earliest time Helen Hughes can remember, her grandmother possessed the gifts of clairvoyance and clairaudience. Apparently, however, she did not recognise these gifts for what they were. To her - as to so many other people in those days - it was simply "second sight," something of a curiosity, but not one which anyone ever attempted to analyse. Her relatives and neighbours, indeed, merely regarded her vaguely as "weird," and left the matter at that. She continually recounted to them the things she claimed to have heard and seen - and, as Helen remembers, she was seldom wrong. Familiarity with these symptoms of "second sight" bred, not contempt, but a placid and uninquiring acceptance of the queer but incomprehensible.

Jane Helen Shepherd, as the granddaughter was christened, was less than a year old when her first brother was born. Her grandmother, who lived nearby, in Maria Street, took her "to stay for a fortnight" . . . and ended by keeping her, and bringing her up, until she left the house to be married.

Although Helen was guided and influenced by her grandmother throughout her childhood days, she learned nothing of the nature of this psychic gift which, it should have soon been apparent, she also shared.

Her parents were Methodists, and the idea that their daughter was a natural psychic did not for one moment occur to them. It is doubtful whether they even knew the meaning of the word. Despite the many proofs of her grandmother's gift, they failed to draw the obvious conclusion that it had been transmitted to their daughter. On the contrary, they secretly entertained serious fears for her sanity, and when she described her invisible playmates, her mother often scolded her for indulging in "absurd fancies." Nevertheless, from her earliest days these spirit children were her constant companions. She has often described how they came into the house, though both front and back doors were locked. This is how she recalls it:

"I have always been able to 'tune in' to the other world - this other dimension beyond time and space. I was taught like other children to sing, 'There is a happy land, far, far away,' but it wasn't far, far away at all to me.

"My mother many times checked me for 'telling lies,' as she called it, about the little girls who were playing with me, and who came into the house though the doors were locked. But the lovely sights of this Other World were always there."

Even at school she was punished for "seeing things," yet - *mirabile dicta!* - a number of other children shared one of the most striking psychic visions of her childhood.

This was when she was eleven years of age, and attending the Seaham Harbour National School. While she was on her way to morning school, and passing through a doorway, she suddenly saw a child - unlike any of those attending the school - inside her classroom, standing beside the window.

Helen called about twelve other children round her and pointed out the child - whom they all declared they could see. They had decided among themselves that the child must have been accidentally locked inside the school when the teacher approached, rather angry at their excited chattering, and the vision disappeared.

Incoherent explanations failed to convince the teacher, who ended by selecting poor little Helen as the "ringleader" of a childish practical joke. As a punishment for "seeing a ghost," she made Helen stand beside the window where the vision of the child had appeared.

It was not the first time that a medium had been victimised for exercising her powers. A few years ago, however, when Helen Hughes was demonstrating at Glasgow, there was a remarkable sequel. The same teacher appeared to her clairvoyantly and said - probably with some contrition: "Well, Nellie Shepherd, so all this began with the ghost!"

About three years after the schoolroom incident, Helen had another outstanding psychic experience.

She was playing in the street with some other children when she suddenly told them to look up at the sky, where, she said, she could clearly see the words, "fever spreading." The other children could see nothing unusual.

Helen's mother, having overheard her remark, called her indoors with a mild rebuke. But three weeks later, Helen herself contracted fever.

She left school not long afterwards, and served her time as an apprentice to a dressmaker - Madame Willoughby - in Church Street, Seaham Harbour, with whom she remained for one year. She then went as an "improver" to the Havelock House, a large firm of drapers, whose premises have since been converted into the Havelock Picture House.

An incident which lingers in her memory from about this time concerns a strange premonition on her part which was the means of saving her brother Harry from probable injury or death. This is how she relates it:

"One morning as my brother Harry was leaving for work, I felt uneasy. As he shut the door behind him, I grew alarmed, and ran to the door and called down the street: 'Don't go to work, Harry - you will be killed.' Though he knew little of Spiritualism, he stayed at home. That morning a machine fell on the boy who took Harry's place and broke both his legs!"

There were no other noteworthy events in her life until the age of eighteen, when she married Thomas Hughes, a miner at the Dawdon Colliery, whom she had known since she was fourteen. They were married at Sunderland, and after living for some time, at Southwick, moved to a small house at Dawdon.

For a time, the responsibilities of married life drove the thought of her psychic experiences into the background. "I have led the ordinary working-woman's life," she once said. "I know all about the difficulties of making ends meet - of bringing up a family on a small income. My feet are well planted on the ground, and my batch of home-made bread will take some beating."

She had three children in just under four years - before she was twenty-two - Vera, Mary and George. Upon the birth of the last baby she developed a severe spinal complaint, and became an invalid with no immediate hope of recovery.

It was then that she passed through the darkest and most difficult days of her life, clouded by pain and physical sickness, and overshadowed by a growing fear of the inexplicable psychic manifestations which now began crowding in upon her, until she began to doubt her sanity. There was no one to explain to her the simple fact, which a Spiritualist could have made clear in a few moments, that she was developing into a medium.

There was, indeed, one dramatic vision of "the shape of things to come" which, had she fully understood it at the time, might have inspired and enlightened her.

"Of the many experiences that came to me at this time one is outstanding," she afterwards wrote, "for it happened when I was near the portals of death, and my friends sat around me waiting for the 'passing.'

"I found myself walking in a garden of dazzling beauty, profuse with flowers and colours, many of which I had never seen before, when I met an elderly lady friend whom I knew to be long since dead.

"How surprised I was to find her alive, and in excitement and joy I spoke to her about the mystery and beauty of it all. I was conscious of a new lease of life - such a contrast to life in the inert physical body.

"After a few moments of conversation, I sighted a flower that even in this garden of ineffable beauty seemed to outshine all in its brilliance of colour, and reached forward to caress it. But I was restrained with the words, *'Not yet, you have work to do!'*

"Then I awoke to find my earth friends bending anxiously over me. Immediately I told them that *I now knew I was not going to die.* They agreed, but, I knew, with doubt in their hearts.

"In later years I learned from my spirit friends that if I had touched that beautiful flower, I would never have returned to physical consciousness. In actuality, that flower symbolised the life of beauty and joy, the spiritual heritage that the soul longed to claim. Had I expressed my emotion by touching that flower, the last link with the physical world would have been severed."

For fully two years after this she was unable to walk, and had to go about in a bath-chair. Many Seaham Harbour residents remember her as she was in those days, worn with pain but enduring her suffering with a cheerful smile and a friendly word for those she met.

It was when she was twenty-three that her latent powers finally asserted themselves. As she lay helpless, she began to hear voices and to see people whom she knew were long-since dead. This at first only alarmed her and filled her with the unreasoning anxiety that her sanity was breaking down under the long strain of illness.

"St. Joan of Arc had heard voices, I knew," she recalls, "but that didn't give me much comfort or help. I was distracted by the voices, and could neither explain them myself nor get anyone else to explain them to me. No doctor could understand or help me, though I was taken to many."

She spent many days - and sometimes nights - of doubt and despondency, mystified as to why she was so different from other people, little reflecting that it is the people who are "different" who lead the world.

She had a startling and impressive visitation when her son George was two or three years old. He became seriously ill, and the doctor diagnosed pneumonia. Mr. and Mrs. Hughes were very alarmed.

"That night," remembers Helen Hughes, "I had a remarkable vision. I saw the form of an Egyptian standing at the boy's head. He took something from a bag resembling balls of cotton wool and held them to the boy's mouth, nose and palms. Then I heard him say, 'A dose of castor oil.' I knew it was dangerous to give him this dose, but I did so, and the next morning he appeared to be quite better.

"When the doctor arrived he exclaimed: 'What can this be? This boy is fit to get up.' But I did not tell him anything about the apparition. I knew he would not have believed me."

With the gradual improvement of her health came an accentuation of the phenomena, and, for the first time, a definite indication of the work she was destined to do in the world, and of the help she was to receive.

She recovered the use of her legs through the encouragement of her "voices," which told her imperatively to "get up and walk."

She could not walk at the time - or she thought she could not - but obedient to the call of the unknown she determined to try. This episode may best be described in her own words:

"I heard voices continually calling, 'Get up and walk.' I could not walk at that time, but I tried, and found when I put my feet on the floor they had life in them, though they seemed to have been dead for a long time.

"With perseverance I began to walk, and it was at this time that I began to realise what Spiritualism really meant. But the significant thing was that, because I was always telling others about the voices I heard, I was thought to be going insane."

When the doctor called again, she repeated what the voices had told her. He knew nothing of psychic matters, and, believing her mind might become unhinged, advised her to go away for a rest. But Helen Hughes was becoming inspired with a growing confidence in herself, and felt instinctively that she had turned the corner. Trusting in her "voices," she persisted in her efforts, and, after walking for some time with the aid of sticks, was eventually able to discard them.

As she grew better, the voices became stronger, louder and more frequent. They were accompanied by other manifestations, which she was later able to understand, but which, at the time, were extraordinarily disconcerting. There were knockings on the wall, the bed would shake, and the bedclothes were sometimes snatched off her at night!

Despite her belief in the voices, she was terrified, and assumed that the house must be "haunted." Whenever anyone called, she could not resist telling them about the disturbances, but they only stared at her incredulously. All the sympathy she received from one neighbour was the remark, "You must have a funny conscience.

About this time she was frequently visited by the form of an unknown woman, whom she saw quite clearly, but who did not speak to her. These visits continued for months. Often she spent restless and disturbed nights, punctuated by knockings and voices - which, however, repeatedly assured her that she was going to get well.

Eventually she begged her husband to move to another house. He was naturally sympathetic and concerned, but almost as incredulous as the neighbours, and insisted that there was nothing wrong with the house. At length she decided to go to the colliery office, where, in company with her husband, she interviewed the under-manager, Mr. Thomas Liddell. He proved unexpectedly understanding and helpful.

She frankly described her experiences, expecting ridicule, but determined to escape from the "haunted" house.

"Please don't think I am insane," she implored him.

He was the first person to display real appreciation of her difficulties. "You are not insane," he declared with a friendly smile. Turning to Mr. Hughes, he remarked: "There is more in her little finger, than in some people's whole bodies." It transpired that his wife was a Spiritualist, and that he understood something of the subject, but unfortunately he did not explain this fact to Helen Hughes at the time. She had to wait several months before she at last learned the truth about her psychic powers.

However, the under-manager found her a new house, "Embankment Cottage," close by, and there the matter ended so far as he was concerned.

If she believed that a change of residence would free her from the strange influences surrounding her, she was speedily undeceived. They followed her to her new home, and became more insistent than ever. But the change brought one important if unexpected development. Mr. Hughes, who still chaffingly insisted that she was "seeing things," began to see things himself!

He hoped that their removal to a new home would end the manifestations. He soon realised that they were centred round his wife and not the house, and, furthermore, that they were real, and not the figments of her imagination. He saw sufficient to convince him that there were more things in Dawdon than had been dreamed of in their philosophy.

The apparition of the "dead" woman persisted. Helen Hughes told her neighbours that the woman was "haunting" her, and they went away, sagely shaking their heads. Then came the startling climax.

"Have you seen that woman any more?" her husband asked her one night.

When she replied that she had, and that she could feel the woman near her at the very moment, he was dismayed. A few fours later he came to her, awed and astonished, and announced that he himself had seen the woman - this time holding a baby in her arms.

"I'll never more say you are insane," he promised fervently. Neither of them had yet associated their experiences with Spiritualism, nor had any desire to investigate it. Yet the day of their awakening was not far distant.

Helen Hughes 1939

CHAPTER III
THE ROAD-MENDER WHO KNEW

> "And folly, doctor-like controlling skill,
> And simple truth miscall'd simplicity."
> Shakespeare.

> "Millions of spiritual creatures walk the earth
> Unseen, both when we wake and when we sleep."
> Milton, "Paradise Lost."

There is something symbolical in the incident which, opened the eyes of Helen Hughes to the fact of her mediumship. In most communities today, the possession of a psychic gift is quickly identified, even if not encouraged to develop. In the village where she spent her early married life, there were many to discourage and bewilder, and few to guide and advise. Destiny brought an obscure but spiritually enlightened wayfarer to her door to transform her life.

One morning - after she had spent a very restless night because of the "voices" - there came three raps on the door.

She opened it and found standing there an old road-mender, who had been working lust outside. He asked her if she would warm his can of tea at the fire.

When she invited him in, he quickly noticed that she was walking with the aid of a stick. His eyes lighted up with sympathy. "Mistress, what's the matter with thee?" he asked in the Durham dialect.

She told him about her illness, and then hesitated. So many people to whom she had described her visions and voices had looked at her with dull suspicion or pity, but something urged her do confide in the old man.

She explained that her greatest tragedy was the fear of losing her reason, because she saw and heard the "dead."

The house was haunted, she declared, and she could not get away from the strange woman visitant. But the road-mender was warmly interested and reassuring.

"Why, hinney," he exclaimed, "ye're the richest Woman in Dawdon! She has come to do you good, and to help you, and you are going to be a great woman."

Helen Hughes answered that it could never be so, but the old man would not be denied.

"Speak to her," he urged.

"I dare not do that," she objected.

"Give her a good thought," persisted the road-mender. "Realise that she is not dead but is coming to help you."

The road-mender was a Spiritualist, and in a few minutes he told her many things which she had never heard or read before, and which at once elucidated her problem. In simple terms, he explained to her how the so-called dead can communicate with the living.

"You are merely using an extra sense, one that is beyond the ordinary five," he said. "Second sight is what some people call it, but it is really an extra sense which we have not yet developed. In the future it will, be common to us all."

For six months after that, he came to see her daily, encouraging her in every way he could.

"He talked to me about what the spirit friends would do to help me," said Helen Hughes, recalling the episode. "He had the true education of the soul. His simple outdoor life, close to the heart of nature, had given him a knowledge of this other world which most town-dwellers lack.

"Oh, how this good old man encouraged me and brought light to my terror-stricken mind! Those raps at the door still resound in my heart. They were raps of deliverance - of hope.

"And so my mind was set at rest, and then of course my health quickly improved. Just those few little words from that poor, old, unknown roadman led me to the exploration of this other world. He mended me, he smoothed my road, and from that day I was slowly led to become a public demonstrator."

The road-mender advised her to visit a Spiritualist church in Sunderland. His advice led her from the pathway to the highway and the lifelong pilgrimage of mediumship.

It is necessary here to turn back a little, and record the death of her father, of which her mediumistic grandmother had an amazing premonition.

One summer evening in 1914, Helen Hughes and other members of the family who had called to see Mr. and Mrs. Shepherd, then living at Adolphus Street, Seaham Harbour, were discussing a little niece who had been killed by a motor-car at Sunderland, and who was to be buried the next day.

"This is not the end of the trouble," said Mrs. Shepherd sadly. "I will give you not longer than three weeks, or three days perhaps, before someone else in the family dies, and this time it will be a bigger blow." Upon being remonstrated with, the grandmother replied: "You may all smile, but three times I heard the sound of soil being thrown against the bedroom door."

The family tried to laugh away this gloomy premonition, but early the next morning, at five minutes to three, someone knocked at the door to break the news that Henry Shepherd had suddenly collapsed and died after getting up to go to work on the night shift at the glass works.

The death of her husband was a terrible blow to Helen's mother; she went into a decline and died only ten months afterwards - many people said of a broken heart. Helen's father was only forty years of age and her mother thirty-nine. Her grandmother, Mrs. Shepherd, however, lived until the age of seventy-eight, and her grandfather, Mr. George Shepherd, to eighty-six.

Helen Hughes soon recovered sufficiently to be able to travel into Sunderland with her husband to visit a specialist, who was very pleased with her progress.

On one of these visits, while looking into a shop window in Longnewton Street, Mrs. Hughes met a friend from

Dawdon, a Mrs. Tennant, who invited her to a Spiritualist meeting in Sunderland.

Remembering what the old road-mender had said, she accepted the invitation, though with some trepidation. Before the meeting she remarked to Mrs. Tennant, "I hope they won't speak to me," but as it turned out, she received the first message at the meeting.

The medium, a Mr. Clews, whom she had never seen before, not only told Helen Hughes all about her psychic experiences - particularly about the woman who was "haunting" her - but predicted that she would become a great medium.

So impressed was the medium with the psychic forces surrounding Mrs. Hughes that he accompanied her and Mrs. Tennant to the station. His last words before leaving her were: "When you see that woman again, you must speak to her, because she has come to help you. The day is coming when you will travel into three countries with the message of the spirit."

Helen Hughes had not long to wait for her mysterious woman visitant, but this time it was with greater confidence. The spirit visitor came with a dramatic message. This is how Helen Hughes relates it:

"The next time the woman visited me, I saw her coming through my bedroom door with her hands clasped together, and before she reached my bedside I sat up in bed saying: 'I will speak to you! I will speak to you!'

"The woman said to me, 'I am Willie Ducker's mother.' I knew Willie Ducker well, as he lived in the village, but he had been fighting at the front - this was in the first Great War - and had been missing for several months. Mrs. Ducker had been dead a number of years.

"I got up the next morning very excited, and was running over to my grandmother to tell her the woman had spoken to me, when I passed the postman, who had just delivered a letter to Willie's sister.

"As I was passing, she called out, 'Oh, Nellie, our Willie's been killed!'"

"I understood then why Mrs. Ducker had been trying to communicate with me for so long. She must have known what had happened to her son, and wanted to tell me, so that I could inform her family. Looking back, it all seemed simple, and I saw clearly that I need not have been afraid.

"From that time on, I realised that there was more in Spiritualism than I had ever believed."

This unmistakable proof of her mediumship encouraged Helen Hughes to persevere. Mrs. Tennant pressed her to join a small private circle which she and a few friends were forming in Dawdon. Though they did not realise it at the time, this was the foundation of a new Spiritualist church at Seaham Harbour.

The circle created such interest that many other people wanted to join it, and the organisers decided to engage a hall in the council schools. Even this proved inadequate, after a few years, and when sufficient funds had been raised a wooden army but was purchased for £50 and erected at Seaham Harbour.

The hut was eventually demolished, but a shop was taken at Seaham, to be used as a meeting-place, and for a time two active societies existed there. In 1937, they amalgamated and created a building fund, which resulted in the opening of a new Spiritualist church, with accommodation for 600 people, at Vane Road, Seaham Harbour, on February as, 1939.

Among those chiefly instrumental in raising the funds for the church was its president, Mr. John Froude, who was convinced of Survival through the mediumship of Mrs. Hughes, and who worked with great enthusiasm. The church is now regarded as one of the finest and most thriving Spiritualist centres in the country.

In those early days Helen Hughes and her friends little dreamed how far both she and the circle would progress.

Helen Hughes never sat in a "developing circle," as many mediums do in their early stages. This preliminary is not indispensable. Indeed, many powerful mediums have developed more or less spontaneously, and, at the outset, with the accompaniment of manifestations even more startling than those which first disturbed Helen Hughes. The entities on the Other Side are sometimes obliged to resort to rather spectacular means of attracting the attention of, and convincing, potential mediums.

Helen Hughes began by giving clairvoyance at these little meetings, and she, at least, was "not without honour" in her own town, for she speedily established a reputation as a medium. Sitters received amazing proofs of Survival, and Helen Hughes herself found a new and absorbing interest in life. But she never demanded a fee for all her demonstrations at Dawdon and Seaham, and over a period of twenty-one years has given her services free to the church which launched her into public life as a medium.

She was rewarded, at all events, in one important respect, for her health continued steadily to improve. One of the worst symptoms - curvature of the spine - disappeared, and she was able to walk without assistance. The voices and visions were no longer terrifying. Instead, they became an encouragement and an inspiration.

Her husband - fully convinced after his own psychic experience - now joined with her in forming a home circle, which her brother and two sisters, and later her three children, also attended regularly. Visitors were sometimes invited.

Incidentally, all her brothers and sisters have at some time or other had flashes of psychic insight. Mediumship is said to "run in families." Her sister Florence is very psychic, but unfortunately has been rendered an invalid by heart trouble and, though she is clairvoyant and clairaudient, is unable to practise in public. Of Helen Hughes's children, Mary has a strongly developed psychic gift, and has taken the platform at meetings on various occasions, but prefers to work in the family circle. George, too, has inherited the gift, and is stated to have "the makings of a fine medium."

Both Helen Hughes's daughters are married. Mary's married name is Wilson; Vera is now Mrs. Robson.

Two years after the formation of the home circle, Helen Hughes's guides made themselves known. The first to entrance or "control" her was a quaint little personality giving the name of Mazeeta, a six-year-old North American Indian girl. Mazeeta, who, in her seemingly artless way, concentrates largely on evidential facts, has convinced hundreds of sitters.

To the family, Mazeeta exemplified the phrase, "A little child shall lead them," for she provided astonishing evidence. Two striking instances - both of them prophetic - may be quoted.

In the first, Mazeeta told Helen Hughes's married sister that she would give birth to a baby girl on September 14 - a prophecy which was exactly fulfilled.

On the other occasion, when the medium's brother-in-law, in the Navy, was due to return to sea, Mazeeta told him, "You will be back in four days because your boat will be involved in a collision."

He was reproved by an officer for joking about this message on board, but the collision did occur, and he was home again in four days, exactly as Mazeeta had predicted.

Mazeeta controlled Helen Hughes for eleven years, giving messages every week at the home circle.

An important stage in the medium's development was then marked by the advent of White Feather, a North American Indian doctor, who explained that he was in charge of the spirit band working through the medium.

He pronounced his name "Whita" Feather, and came to be familiarly and affectionately addressed as "Whita" for short. Declaring that Mazeeta had taken exclusive possession long enough, he explained that his arrival was part of the medium's psychic evolution, and that he wanted to train her so that he could speak and lecture through her in public. He revealed himself as a philosopher and teacher, propounding the truths of spirit life with a quiet and benign dignity, and with a power of oratory beyond the range of the medium herself.

Mazeeta, of course, still continues to "come through" at intervals, particularly when children are present. Another control also announced herself, in the person of "Grannie Anderson," who once lived in County Durham, and who speaks in a rich local dialect. She is a friendly soul, but only an infrequent visitor, who just "pops in" now and then "to see how things are going on." She announced herself first at a Christmas party, when she explained that she had been attracted that night by e light she saw. She added that her "job" was looking after children in the spirit world - work she found easy and congenial in comparison with her earthly life in which it had been difficult to keep body and soul together.

These "controls" soon manifested at other gatherings, but it should be noted that Helen Hughes seldom goes into trance at public meetings. She finds her clairaudience adequate in most circumstances.

It was at about this period that Helen Hughes unexpectedly met another stranger who, like the roadmender, divined the wealth of her psychic powers.

Following the death of her father, she and her brothers and sisters had combined to run a little restaurant at Green Street, Seaham Harbour. Late one night, after the restaurant had been closed, but apparently while the savoury smell of cooking was still wafted from the windows, there was a knock at the side door.

The caller proved to be a Norwegian sailor, who asked if he could have a meal. This was hospitably provided, and when he had finished it, he suddenly turned to Helen Hughes, whom he had been watching with peculiar intentness, and said in broken English: "Lady, you spew with angels. You are not doing all this alone. You have angel mother Margaret, who tells me she is helping you and your family."

The mysterious sailor was a complete stranger to Helen Hughes, but this message made her more determined than ever to work for Spiritualism.

Although she began her career as a medium by giving clairvoyance at the small meetings at Seaham, and had no thought of going further afield, it was not long before the quality of her mediumship began to attract wider attention.

Once, when the speaker failed to appear, she decided to take the whole meeting, and was so successful that subsequently the church officials were never concerned whether she had a speaker with her or not. She began to carry on these meetings at the Seaham Harbour Church single-handed in 1926, during the General Strike. Her audiences, averaging about 250 people, would hear her read from the Bible - or she was not a fluent speaker - before giving a demonstration of clairaudience. In addition, 'she began to tour the county of Durham, where there is scarcely a Spiritualist church which she has not visited.

She declares that at all times during the early stages of her public mediumship she could sense the presence of her mother - the "Margaret" to whom the psychic sailor had referred.

From the foundation of the church at Seaham Harbour, Helen Hughes was placed on the roll of official lecturer-mediums of the Northern District Council of the Spiritualists' National Union. After about ten years' work at this church, the members presented her with a gold watch in recognition of her services.

Then, in 1929, came an invitation to enter a wider field. It was from Mr. J. B. McIndoe (treasurer and past-president of the Spiritualists' National Union) asking her to visit the Holland Street Spiritualist Church, Glasgow. She did not wish to leave her home, but eventually, urged by her spirit guides, she accepted the invitation. "From that day," she says, "I never seemed to be out of Scotland, whose people I love very much."

Actually, the first Spiritualist church in Scotland at which she demonstrated was at Gayfield Square, Edinburgh, which she visited shortly before travelling to Glasgow.

Needless to add, the Spiritualists of Scotland love Helen Hughes. She is a frequent and eagerly - awaited visitor to the Edinburgh Psychic College in Heriot Row, at the St. Vincent Street Church and the St. Andrew's Hall, Glasgow, and other centres in Scotland.

Since her first visit to Scotland she has journeyed thousands of miles, delivering messages to thousands of sitters in England, Scotland, Ireland and Wales. The prediction that she would "travel into three countries with the message of the spirit" has therefore been amply fulfilled.

HELEN HUGHES

CHAPTER IV
PRAISE FROM THE PRESS

"The report of my death was an exaggeration."
Mark Twain, Letter 1897.

"There is no death! What seems so is transition."
Longfellow.

I never cease to marvel that I have become well known," said Helen Hughes in conversation one day. Spiritualists never cease to, marvel that she is, not even better known. If, the world realised their value, as our only link with that unseen but nevertheless real world beyond our normal range of perception, mediums would be honoured and extolled - not ridiculed, misrepresented and neglected as they are by the public at large. In years to come, I believe, statues will be erected to such mediums as Helen Hughes, and their names will go down in psychic history.

Helen Hughes travels thousands of miles every year to appear on public platforms all over Great Britain. To Spiritualists she is a public figure. Her simplicity and approachability are in keeping with the spirit of the movement. Admiration cannot mar her modesty nor custom stale her infinite variety. Although, in the opinion of Spiritualists, mediums are of infinitely greater value than all the priesthood, they are happily not surrounded by the satellites and ceremonies, the trappings and the trumpetings, and the sanctimonious, solemn mumbo jumbo with which most of the dignitaries of the Church are propped and palisaded and isolated from the people, and which serve only to obscure the sterility of their teachings.

I would back Helen Hughes against the whole bench of bishops in a brains trust on the survival of man. While the Church stagnates and reiterates, and science prevaricates, the medium demonstrates. To see Helen Hughes on the public platform is to witness an object-lesson in realism.

"No medium in Britain is in greater demand for public platform work than Helen Hughes of Dalton-le-Dale. In Dublin, Belfast, Glasgow, Edinburgh, Sheffield and Manchester she has often addressed public meetings of as many as 3,000 people."

I quote this paragraph, from an article in the "Sunday Sun," Newcastle-on-Tyne, June 19, 1938, as typical of the praise accorded by the unbiased Press for the platform work of Helen Hughes.

This article was written, under the name of "Maxwell Scott," by a Newcastle man - not a Spiritualist - whom I know well, and for whose opinions I have the greatest respect. In a series of articles for the "Sunday Sun" entitled "Spiritualism in the North," he wrote a graphic summary of the life of Helen Hughes.

The "Sunday Sun" treated the subject with scrupulous fairness, and the series aroused wide interest. Incidentally there are thousands of people today who are "interested" in Spiritualism and who believe that there is "something in it" without troubling to inquire into it more closely. I have met many of these "half-convinced" people, who would be glad to learn more of the subject, but - it is worthy of recording - I have met none who, after receiving evidence from Helen Hughes, have not been fully convinced of the genuineness of her mediumship.

The Press as a whole is decidedly cautious and non-committal in reporting mediumistic demonstrations, but occasionally, when recording those of Helen Hughes, even the ranks of Tuscany can scarce forbear to cheer. As "Light," one of the journals of Spiritualism, somewhat naively remarked of the Sixth International Spiritualist Congress meetings at the St. Andrew's Hall, Glasgow, in September, 1937, when Helen Hughes, among other mediums, again triumphed, "Even the representatives of the daily papers were favourably impressed, as their descriptions of the proceedings indicated."

The "Two Worlds," another Spiritualist journal, stated, "It has been the most wonderful Press Spiritualism has ever known." Needless to say, the Spiritualist Press is lavish in its praises for the platform work of this remarkable medium. Here are some quotations which reflect her popularity:

"Psychic News," April 29 and May 6, 1944: "At this meeting Helen Hughes will demonstrate the superb mediumship that has made her famous all over the country. Throughout the land crowds flock to meetings when they see that Helen Hughes is announced to demonstrate her brilliant mediumship. She has earned her place in the front rank by the irrefutable evidence she gives at all her demonstrations."

The "Two Worlds" (reporting a meeting at the Bath Spiritualist Church): "Full names, degrees of relationship and incidents in the past lives of the spirit communicators were given to various members of the audience. Throughout the whole of the clairvoyance there was not a single description which was not fully recognised." (Meeting at Baker St. Church, Doncaster) "In less than forty minutes she gave descriptions to over twenty people. Sixty-six names were given." (Meeting at Leven, Fife): "Nearly 500 people packed the Masonic Hall to listen to Mr. W. Lorraine Haig, secretary of the Scottish D.C., speak... but in particular to watch and gasp at the demonstration of clairaudient mediumship presented by Mrs. Helen Hughes. For 45 minutes she kept the audience tense by her amazing gift"

Programmes for meetings at the Usher Hall, Edinburgh, gave the following description of Helen Hughes:

"She may be regarded as one of the most outstanding witnesses to the actuality of spiritual existence of this age. To this work she has given herself with a self-sacrificing devotion and love for her fellow-beings which have made her one of the "most esteemed ministrants of her time. Her messages are direct and accurate to an extraordinary degree.... She has brought consolation and assurance of continuing life to many homes '-which have suffered bereavement by the war. Her work during this period gives her a high place in the modern history of psychic 'science. Her experiences have included many dramatic and impressive incidents, and the accuracy of her messages and the actuality of their source have been established by the abundant witness of grateful recipients all over the country."

In her own area, Helen Hughes is well received by the Press. To quote the "Sunday Sun" again (reporting a meeting at Newcastle City Hall in October, 1934): "The huge audience audibly gasped as listener after listener acknowledged the accuracy of her statements."

One reporter, in the "Kilmarnock Standard," describing his first Spiritualist meeting, was warm in his praises of Helen Hughes, though - possibly to safeguard himself from criticism - he ended his account with a bald ambiguity.

The meeting was held by the Kilmarnock Spiritualist Association at the Grand Hall, with an audience of nearly 1500 people. Describing Helen Hughes, the reporter wrote: "She is of a distinctly superior type; her appearance would attract attention in any company in which she was; in her facial expression there is refinement, gentleness, spiritual beauty, and the tones of her voice convey the same suggestion....

"It was an emotionally disturbing experience, the more so that there was no suggestion of theatricality in the attitude of the medium. While addressing her audience she spoke in a natural, unaffected way - there was no posturing or attempt at dramatisation.

"But suddenly a tenseness would come into her manner - she seemed to be listening, and sometimes she would murmur as to someone by her side or just above her, 'Yes, all right,' and then announce a name to the audience."

The reporter (or could this have been a sub-editorial addendum?) concluded with the remark that the demonstration did not prove the existence of a spirit world, and that "it could as readily be interpreted as the result of an abnormal brain condition.

Precisely what such a "brain condition" could be there was no attempt to define.

"Maxwell Scott" wrote of Helen Hughes: "London knows her best, for her demonstrations of clairvoyance at the Caxton Hall are attended by hundreds of inquirers. From Society folk came invitations for Helen Hughes to stay with them at their castles and their mansions. And, at the other end of the scale - but no less valuable - is her work for mourners who are unable to pay any fee for the proofs they seek.

"To thousands of people in all walks of life, Mrs. Hughes is giving complete proof of Survival."

He also testified as follows to the "good Press" which Helen Hughes has received: "I have read through a collection of Press cuttings taken from scores of newspapers throughout the land, and the evidence she has given has been extraordinarily good. Again and again from well-known public figures comes the tribute, 'Britain's greatest public medium.'"

For those who allege that mediums such as Helen Hughes somehow or other collect facts regarding sitters beforehand, the following record should be provocative.

Once, in Ayrshire - a district which she had never visited before - Helen Hughes agreed to meet a motor-car that would take her to a public meeting at an unknown destination. At that meeting she gave more than a score of names and addresses.

On a visit to Belfast, at a meeting attended by over a thousand people, she made a deep impression - though it was a simple enough feat for her - by mentioning the names of more than a score of Ulster people on the Other Side, none of whom she had ever heard of.

Not only did she give their full names but, in several cases, their full addresses and many other particulars.

"*What* a memory I should need!" she exclaimed once, when we were discussing that threadbare allegation that her messages are given by means of collusion with sitters. If there ever had been collusion, one may well ask how it is that not one complaint has ever been made regarding her; not one person has ever come forward to say, "This message was false," or "That message was prearranged." There has never been the faintest breath of condemnation.

Helen Hughes always has remarkable success in repeating names given by spirit communicators. At a Caxton Hall meeting in April, 1937, for instance, she gave dozens of names, some of them unusual ones such as Safonia.

Before Mrs. Hughes could appear on the public platform, she had to overcome many difficulties. Among these were her limited vocabulary and her complete inexperience of public speaking.

These difficulties, with the quiet determination which she has always displayed, she successfully overcame. She studied her school books again, and took lessons in elocution. Her voice is not a strong one, but she was resolved to make the best use of it. Although she is no orator - and makes no pretensions to be one - she often delivers a homely but pointed and effective little address before beginning her demonstrations. In delivering messages - for the speed of which she is noted - she expresses herself fluently, yet with an economy and avoidance of repetition which many other demonstrators and speakers might well emulate.

Recalling how she studied to equip herself for her task, Mrs. Hughes says: "If you had peeped into my cosy sitting room some dark winter's evenings, you would have seen my children sitting at their lessons on one side of the table, and mother on the other side, struggling with her old school books, learning how to pronounce certain words, and how to make a sentence run evenly, all of which was very necessary for me if I was to work successfully in public."

Helen Hughes has done more to educate herself than many mediums with greater opportunities, some of whom, paradoxically enough, show little interest in the meaning of their mediumship. She displays an intelligent interest in both the technical and the spiritual sides of her work, and, having much to teach, is a ways ready to learn. She, too, like her friend the road-mender, possesses the true "education of the soul."

More than once, non-Spiritualists have presided at her meetings. Civic dignitaries, who speak at so many public functions to whose objects they do not necessarily subscribe, sometimes dare to mount even the Spiritualist platform.

Helen Hughes received a particularly kind send-off at a propaganda meeting in the Bensham Picture Hall, Gateshead, in October, 1936. Councillor J. H. Ritson, J.P. (whom I knew well as Alderman Ritson, Mayor of Gateshead) was an impartial chairman. While he was not a Spiritualist, he said, he had been a wide reader. Many of the problems of the universe were still unsolved, but the greatest of all was, "Shall we live hereafter?" That thought had dominated human inquiry throughout history Christianity averred Survival, and placed it on a basis of faith. Spiritualism claimed that it could offer proof, and in his opinion an ounce of fact was worth a ton of theory.

Would that all non-Spiritualists were as intelligent and open-minded as this!

Those who love to malign Spiritualism are fond of asserting that the subject induces mental disorders among its devotees. This is a malicious libel. Statistics completely disprove such childish perversion of the truth. Far from causing mental derangement, Spiritualism has actually saved the reason of many sufferers, and could save many more if the subject were better understood and applied.

Helen Hughes herself has cheered countless mourners, and almost unquestionably saved one mother - tortured by the loss of her three sons in the war - from mental breakdown. This is how Mrs. Hughes related the incident to me:

"One day at St. Vincent Street, Glasgow, Spiritualist Church, a lady came in looking very distracted, dressed in furs, but wearing only carpet-slippers on her feet. She rushed up to me and exclaimed in anguished tones, 'You can tell me where my boys are, if they are dead or living.'

"A moment later her daughter followed her into the church and tried to persuade her to go home, remarking to me, 'She mustn't have anything to do with it.' Apparently her mother had heard of the Spiritualist church, had suddenly made up her mind to visit it, and had run out of the house even without waiting to put on her shoes.

"I asked the daughter to leave her mother in my hands, and promised that I would do her no harm. I made a point of seeing her regularly every day until she became a sane and happy woman again.

"Through the direct contact I established with them, I was able to prove to her that the boys she had thought were dead were now reunited with her. The last time I saw her she said, 'Thank God for such a person as Helen Hughes.'"

An outstanding incident in Mrs. Hughes's platform career was the experiment in which she co-operated for making a gramophone record of a psychic demonstration.

This was at the International Spiritualist Congress, Glasgow, in 1937. Some newspapers reported at the time that she was "making Spiritualist history" with "the first gramophone record of psychic sounds," but gramophone records of séances had been made before this on several occasions. It was, however, so far as I know, the first record made of a public demonstration of clairaudience, and definitely the first made by Helen Hughes.

Mrs. Hughes attached to the shoulder of her dress a small microphone, by means of which every message she gave was relayed to another room and reproduced on the record.

A new apparatus, "The Phono-disc Portable Recording Gramophone," had then recently appeared on the market. It made mechanical recording possible under almost any conditions, and it was considered that recordings of séances, reproducing the distinctive inflections and mannerisms of speech of spirit communicators, would be more valuable in many respects - than ordinary written notes.

About seventy feet of flex was led from the microphone to a room behind the platform where the recording machine was installed. The record, which was broadcast through loudspeakers to the audience on the following day, was made by Mr. Harold B. Miller, and among those who also took an interest in the recording "behind the scenes" was Mr. F. H. Wood, Doctor of Music, of Durham University, and organist of Blackpool Parish Church.

Earlier in the afternoon a private experiment with the phono-disc was made, when Mrs. Hughes went into trance, and conversations were recorded with White Feather and Mazeeta.

At the public demonstration which was recorded, Mrs. Hughes gave over thirty descriptions to the audience, all of which were dearly recognised and acknowledged as correct.

Some remarks which Helen Hughes made on the recording are of interest.

"Experiments in recording psychic sounds, it is true, are in their infancy," she said, "but I have no hesitation in stating that with the widespread use of gramophone recording, much outstanding evidence that would otherwise be lost will now be preserved permanently.

"Furthermore, I hope that by means of gramophone records, important new discoveries will be made. The camera has accomplished much by registering visible or normally invisible phenomena. The recording gramophone can accomplish even more in the realm of psychic sound."

It was hoped at the time that the experiment might be widely imitated, as it was claimed that the apparatus was comparatively inexpensive. There is certainly a case for more regular and methodical recording of demonstrations and séances, but certain difficulties exist. Stenographers and scientific apparatus are not always obtainable. Records - whether written or on gramophone discs - are valuable for reference or as evidence: gramophone records have the especial value that they can be re-played many times, thus providing the basis of detailed critical study; but apart from this, they have certain limitations. Sceptics, who disbelieve what they hear about séances, are not likely to be convinced by typewritten notes or gramophone records, which they can easily allege to be concocted or faked. However, there is definitely room for more science in the séance-room.

To mention one instance of methodical work, the West Riding Psychical Society, Bradford, kept a careful record of all Helen Hughes's visits from 1929 to 1932. Her phenomena were stated to be "extremely impressive throughout." Subsequently she was introduced to Mr. O. J. Wendlandt (secretary of the Sheffield Society for Psychical Research), and also to Mrs. Rose Champion de Crespigny, president of the British College of Psychic Science, who has now passed on.

As a point of interest, Rose de Crespigny spoke through Helen Hughes, in trance, at the Edinburgh Psychic College in January 1945. Several sitters who knew this woman well claimed to recognise her mannerisms and mode of speech.

Another point of interest is that Mrs. Hughes's first meeting outside her own county was at Harrogate. Her first propaganda meeting was at Bristol, where, it is recorded, she caused a sensation.

In the course of her travels up and down the country, Helen Hughes has endured many discomforts, but has had few mishaps. Some years ago, she had a narrow escape from possible death - not because of a premonition, but by chance - when she just missed a train which was subsequently wrecked.

She was travelling from King's Cross to Newcastle, but owing to the length of time the porter took in bringing - her luggage from the taxi, she missed the train. Shortly afterwards it was wrecked at Welwyn Garden City, and many passengers were killed or injured.

During her long years of platform work, Helen Hughes has travelled thousands of miles by land, sea and air. She has visited most of the principal towns and cities in England and Scotland, and has also toured Wales and parts of Ireland. She has addressed audiences of up to 4,000 people.

"I have spoken in Ireland in the afternoon and in Scotland the same night," she told me. "I have travelled by aeroplane several times, and will do it again. I have not spared myself once. The spirit people chose me, and I have tried to serve them."

"Is there any medium who travels more miles to demonstrate her psychic gifts than Helen Hughes?" asked "Psychic News" on December 11, 1943. "Churches outside London which clamour for well-known mediums to visit them do not always appreciate the strain involved in wartime travelling. Helen Hughes was telling us the other day how it took her twelve hours to go from Newcastle-on-Tyne to Birmingham. She had to stand in the corridor, or sit on her suitcase all the way. Her only relief was at two stations where she had to change and where she got very light meals. Helen treats it all as part of her war work.

Helen Hughes has delivered innumerable messages to people from all over the country - and some of them have travelled equally long distances to see her. One visitor came all the way from Aberdeen to London for a private sitting.

She has met many celebrities interested in Spiritualism, and among her friends she numbers Air Chief Marshal Lord Dowding (Head of Fighter Command in the Battle of Britain), Nina Duchess of Hamilton (well known throughout Britain for her philanthropic work), Hannen Swaffer, Arthur Findlay, Vice-Admiral Armstrong and Miss Lind-af-Hageby (the well-known worker for humanitarian causes and international friendship).

In her own area, she has visited almost every Spiritualist church in County Durham, and in Northumberland has demonstrated at Newcastle, Whitley Bay, North Shields, Blyth, Ashington, Newbiggin and other towns.

In his summing-up of "Spiritualism in the North," my friend "Maxwell Scott" wrote, "Where formerly I had faith in Survival, I now have proof." He admitted that before he began his inquiry he shared with thousands of people many preconceived notions on the subject.

Referring to Helen Hughes, he said: "I do, not believe that clairvoyance is the result of telepathy or inquiry by the medium. The evidential message from Helen Hughes about my hospital friend Jack Wilson contained references that are known only to a few people. Mrs. Hughes could not have known anything about them. (See Chapter VI.)

"I reject the telepathy explanation, and defy anyone to read my mind.

"Mrs. Hughes travels all over Britain giving hundreds of these evidential messages a week. The suggestion that they are the result of previous inquiry is absurd.

"I have ceased to be surprised," he added, "at the large number of sane, intelligent men of affairs who are Spiritualists."

HELEN HUGHES

CHAPTER V
"SPEAKING IN TONGUES"

Sir Patrick. Do you hear voices?
Ridgeon. No.
Sir Patrick. I'm glad of that. When my patients tell me that they've made a greater discovery than Harvey, and that they hear voices, I lock them up.
      Bernard Shaw, "The Doctor's Dilemma."

Some details of the nature of Helen Hughes's mediumship and of her guides will be of interest to the reader at this stage.

Helen Hughes has contributed more substantially than most mediums to the steadily accumulating mass of evidence for Survival, but she often stresses, modestly, that she is only the instrument of higher powers, and that much of her work is done on the Other Side.

People who expect to be told precisely what mediumship is, "how it works," and how it can be proved, are demanding little less than the solution of one of the riddles of the universe. Mediums, as a rule, do not profess to "prove" anything, to the public. They demonstrate their psychic powers, and leave intelligent listeners to form their own conclusions. In the case of Helen Hughes, thousands of sitters - many of whom were formerly sceptics - have been convinced that Survival is a fact.

The chief objection of many sceptics - even though they subscribe to orthodox doctrines which proclaim Immortality - is, "How can we communicate with people if they are dead?" We certainly could not communicate with them if they really were dead, but the fact is that they are not dead, but living on a different plane of existence.

To put it another way, they have passed to a different rate of vibration. For a truly illuminating scientific exposition of this fact, I recommend the reader to Arthur Findlay's "On the Edge of the Etheric," and "The Unfolding Universe." There is no "resting until the resurrection" The grave is not the goal, and life is real and earnest, as never before, at the end of our earthly span.

A simple outline of the basis of mediumship was once given by the Rev. Drayton Thomas, in introducing Mrs. Hughes to a meeting at the Caxton Hall, London.

"Each of our five senses can be extended in range and delicacy," he said, "but we must not suppose that Mrs. Hughes will be dependent on her eyes or ears for anything she will tell us.

"In addition to the five senses there is another avenue by which information reaches the sensitive . . . the sixth sense. We shall be on sure ground if we call it psychic sensing. Psychically gifted persons can, to some extent, see and hear that which is invisible and inaudible to others; this is not on account of having more sensitive eyes and ears, but owing to the fact that they are able to use a special sense.

"I believe it is a sensing by the etheric body. We each live in such a body, and it may be that it is interpenetrating, cell by cell, this familiar body of flesh . . . and it is probably the intermediary between the soul, or self, and the physical body. We pass from earth in that ethereal body at death, and it will then bring us into touch with the Beyond as ingeniously as this body with its five senses brings us into touch with' the earth.

"Some are so constituted that they are able to use it now, at least to some degree, in seeing and hearing those who visit us from the Beyond, and when these gifted people tell us what they see and hear, they are intermediaries between us and our discarnate friends.

"Visitants from the other world can do nothing to indicate their presence unless we provide the necessary means. The indispensable requisite is some form of psychic energy. The silence of death can only be broken by such indications and messages as mediums are able to convey to us from those whose continued love prompts them to visit us, and to speak if we give them the opportunity."

This is how Helen Hughes described her mediumship, in an article in the "Two Worlds":

"We can attempt to diagnose our feelings in the various phases of demonstration, and yet know very little of the forces in operation and how they are being employed. It seems that in psychic demonstration we are being introduced to a wider range of human faculty, and what is now peculiar to the few may be common to the races of the future.

"My own mediumship includes clairvoyance, clairaudience and trance. In clairvoyance I see a spirit form as naturally as if I were using the physical eye. I am not aware of any abnormal sensation until I begin to respond to the feelings or characteristics of the spirit that appears to me. These sensations may be of happiness or sorrow, anxiety or peace, and sometimes I find myself responding to the last sensations the spirit experienced before leaving the physical body.

"It appears that by coming into contact with the earth atmosphere there is an association of the old ideas and impressions, causing the last earth experiences of the spirit to recur temporarily. But all these feelings seem to be under the control of my will. That is, I can 'close up' or 'open out' at will. If a sensation is too unpleasant I can 'switch' it off.

"I can often get a clear understanding of the mission and message of the spirit by interpreting these sensations. But it is on my gift of clairaudience that I mostly depend in my demonstrations of Survival. In clairaudience I hear quite naturally, as though I were using the normal ear. The voices sound quite normal. I can tell if it is the voice of a man, woman or child, or if it is a loud voice or a quiet one. Even the characteristics of intonation and modulation are quite noticeable.

"It is listening to the 'voice' that enables me to give the names, facts and details that provide the evidence.

"You may ask: 'If there is such a clear means of communication as this, why are mistakes made? Why is each message not perfect and conclusive?' The answer is, 'The imperfection of the receiving instrument.' The spirit people may be 'broadcasting' the most conclusive evidence and yet the medium hears nothing, or only part of what has been spoken. We are dependent on laws of attunement of which we know little. Even our telephone system has its temporary defects. Can we wonder at the difficulties encountered in trying to communicate with a world of a different dimension?

"I must mention that when these faculties are working strongly, especially in a large and enthusiastic public meeting, I experience a quickening of my whole personality which at times amounts to a feeling of exaltation. It is as though I am flooded with abnormal energies. When this 'power' is strong my faculties of clairvoyance and clairaudience are accelerate It is the 'bridge between the two worlds.' In a sympathetic audience the 'power' is strongest; music and enthusiasm stimulate it.

"Demonstrating in private circles has certain advantages over public meetings. In public there is the obvious difficulty of 'locating' the recipient, and the fact that there are so many eager spirits seeking to communicate. When giving clairaudience in larger gatherings, I am generally able to locate who the message is for by seeing a spirit-light resting on the person. This light varies in colour and intensity according to the characteristics and development of the person communicating. The purpose of the spirit world, when giving a clairaudient message, is to give certain small details which form links in a chain of evidence which precludes all suggestions of fraud or telepathy.

"Now I come to the third and last branch of my mediumship, by which I demonstrate the survival of personality - my trance mediumship. I do not usually go into trance in public. I prefer the normal state. While in trance I am unaware of my surroundings, as if in a sound sleep. Just preceding trance I experience a feeling of sleepiness.

"For knowledge of what happens while in trance I am dependent on my friends. I am told there is a complete transformation of my personality. Facts and proofs of Survival are given of which I could have no previous knowledge.

"It appears that while in trance my active consciousness is held in temporary abeyance, and the spirit friends can use my powers of clairvoyance and clairaudience with greater facility. Sometimes my guides will allow a spirit seeking to prove his survival to enter my body and speak direct to his loved ones, but this is left to the discretion of my two main spirit guides and protectors.

"One I know by the name of Mazeeta, an Indian girl, who specialises mainly in giving messages that prove Survival. The other is White Feather who, though at times he gives proofs of the continuity of life, is more concerned with the greater truths of man's spiritual destiny. Whita is the leader of the unseen powers behind my work. He is the philosopher, the teacher and the comforter. Many hearts have been healed by his kindly words. Tolerance and love are his greatest ideals. He is the great moulding influence in my life.

"All these gifts seem quite natural to me. They came unsought by me. At first I did not understand them. Now I realise they have been the greatest blessing in my life. Since giving full expression to these gifts, I have experienced much better health. Spiritually, mentally and physically I feel a better woman.

"My parting advice is - seek the advice of the spirit people in purity of motive. No matter who you are or what you have been, they will not turn you away. Their love and their tolerance is fathomless. They are the harbingers of the better world that is to be."

At various other times Mrs. Hughes has attempted to explain the technical aspects of her mediumship. The organs of spiritual perception, she says, are seated in the spirit body, which interpenetrates and co-exists with the physical body. During earth life, the spirit body is "subjective," but after death it becomes the active and objective body which associates man with his spirit environment.

Thus, in clairaudience she is utilising an organ that normally belongs to the next stage in man's spiritual evolution. In most individuals, this does not function until they leave the physical body at death.

The purpose of her demonstrations is to transmit communications that will provide the recipient with facts and details proving the survival of human personality after death.

Before a demonstration, she makes herself completely passive. She declares that she can "tune in" to the other world at any time. When demonstrating in public she experiences a sense of detachment, and feels as if a force, almost magnetic in nature, is rising from her feet. There seems to her to be something like a series of "telegraph wires," a range of vibrations, along which the messages come. She finds that power for public demonstrations lasts about half an hour. After that time, the power dies down, and as she is then liable to become less accurate, she has to stop. To force the power would be to court inaccuracy, and impose a strain on the system.

In giving clairaudience, she seems to act as a "human radioreceiver," and also, on the comparatively rare occasions on which she can see and describe scenes in the past or the future, as a "televisor."

She actually hears the voices speaking in her ears - or even in the region of the solar plexus - a phenomenon known to other mediums. The voices vary in, clarity, some being as loud as ordinary physical voices and others whispering or in muffled tones.

The following is a summary of an account she once wrote of her reactions "under control":

"Passing under control I would liken to falling asleep. When seeking control, I relax physically and mentally, and am aware of a gradual drugging of my consciousness which reminds me of the sensations accompanying chloroform inhalation.

"Coming out of control I have the same feeling as when awakening from sleep. If the trance has been deep and prolonged, I have the feeling of having arrived back from some distant place.

"This feeling of having travelled is more in evidence after the spirit guides have had what they term 'total possession' of my body. During such times, it appears I am out of my body completely, being only connected with it by the 'life-cord.' The spirit friends inform me that they take this total possession only when my physical body needs special attention and healing, and it is not necessary for the ordinary unconscious trance sitting.

"While in 'total possession' they have often described my spirit activities out of the body, but on returning to normal after trance, I have no recollection whatever of my out-of-the-body experiences.

"After control I generally feel much better. It leaves me with a feeling of renewal, analogous to a glass of water being emptied and refilled with fresh water. My trance experience is quite pleasant. It is preceded by a pleasant feeling of complete relaxation and resignation, and the after-effects are such as follow healthy sleep."

White Feather, who is a Sioux Indian, once explained that he had exerted his spirit influence over her long before he first manifested through her. As he was dealing with a medium of fragile physique, he had to wait until her body was strong enough to bear the strain and fatigue of full mediumship.

"Whita," she says, "claims that the demonstrated facts of Survival would, if universally known, inspire men to build a new world of peace, harmony and sanity.

"The most outstanding characteristic of White Feather I have found to be tolerance towards other people's opinions, and sympathy and charity for the erring one.

"He speaks of the problems of man's origin and spiritual destiny with intellectual, philosophic insight that far transcends my own knowledge and ability. He builds on the proven facts of Survival an interpretation of life and destiny that is both constructive and inspiring. He claims that when the truth of man's spiritual origin and destiny dawns upon mankind, a new world of human relationship will be born. Human values will be revolutionised, mental perspectives will be broadened. Nationalism will give way to universalism and war will be banished from the earth for ever.

"His talks are not just Utopian idealism and sentimentality; he reveals a world of men freed from the blindness of materialism and the cramping creedalism of institutional religion. There is not an idealistic over-accentuation of spiritual development to the neglect of the immediate problems of man's material environment. This must be improved for the development of those budding qualities of mind and spirit that come to fruition in the world beyond death.

"When the truth of Survival and the reality of the existence of the spirit become universally known, hypocrisy, selfishness and injustice will give way to justice and humanity born of the realisation, not only that men are part of a universal brotherhood, but that with a background of immortality, the treasures of the spirit can be the only ultimate value.

"The narrow barriers of life and thought shall be broken down with the realisation of man's undying spiritual nature.

Bridges shall be built across the gulfs of nationality. Property shall not be exalted above the .sacredness of human life and happiness. By the removal of the dogmas of both science and institutional religion, the human intellect, in a new lease of life and liberty, shall make discoveries that will improve the material conditions and uplift the cultural level of the whole race."

With regard to Mazeeta, Helen Hughes says, "My Indian girl control specialises in providing proof of Survival and spirit destiny which precludes any possibility of previous knowledge on my part."

Mazeeta, in addition to being an immortal, appears to be a spiritual Peter Pan, possessing the secret of eternal youth, for despite the fact that she has controlled Helen Hughes for many years, she never "grows up." The explanation, according to Spiritualistic lore, is that, although a spirit child may "grow up" and progress to higher planes, it often reassumes the personality of a child upon contact with the earth conditions.

Helen Hughes was once asked at a meeting, "Do child controls ever grow up?" Her reply was: "Yes, as they ascend to other planes. When they return to the child plane, they behave like children."

The verdict of my friend "Maxwell Scott" regarding Mazeeta was, "The voice of Mazeeta seemed to me to be the genuine voice of a little girl." Grannie Anderson, he wrote, sounded like "a real canny body."

"I can only say," he added, "that if you heard these three voices on your radio you would find it impossible to credit that they could all come from one person. If Mrs. Hughes is not a genuine trance medium, then she could make a fortune giving character impressions on the stage."

Nothing arouses the scorn and suspicion of the sceptic so much as the fact that mediums claim to have Red Indian and other "outlandish" guides. The idea seems to them - fantastic and incongruous - as if Englishmen, or at least white men, were the exclusive occupants of "heaven," i.e., the higher spheres.

It may come as a rude shock to the orthodox to learn that "the heathen of every tribe and nation" are often more highly developed spiritually than their white brothers - partly because of their close contact with nature - and that they are, in consequence, peculiarly fitted to act as guides when they "die."

Possibly if mediums claimed respectable, top-hatted rural deans as guides, it might sound more impressive to the sceptics, but it would seldom be true. The clergy - notwithstanding the many good men among them - have too much to unlearn when they "pass over."

Mediums have nothing to gain, from the point of view of plausibility, by claiming allegiance with "heathen" guides, but they must defy ridicule for the sake of truth. Some of them even have Japanese or German guides. Death, it seems, demolishes many frontiers.

Through the trance mediumship of Helen Hughes, spirits have spoken in perfect conversational French, German, Swedish, Belgian and Portuguese - none of which she knows herself. At one Edinburgh meeting, a Frenchman congratulated her on her perfect grammar and pronunciation, and was astonished to learn that she knew no French.

When she was demonstrating at the International Spiritualist Congress at Glasgow in 1937, she was asked if communications in foreign languages were ever given in trance.

A number of foreigners immediately testified that they had received evidence through her of the continuity of life in their native tongues.

If two or three people respond to a message, Helen Hughes knows which is the right one because when she hears the correct response from the audience, something "clicks" within her. This "click," she says, is caused by the excitement of the spirit communicator at obtaining recognition.

The reason why she often breaks off one message to start another is that the voices do not give her much time. They are rapid, and always break in. Spirit speakers try to use the "vibrations" created by previous communicators.

One exceptionally interesting, though little known "sideline" of Helen Hughes's mediumship is her occasional visits to "haunted" houses.

When newspapers investigate these cases, they usually begin by running a sensational story and end by reporting that "the mystery remains unsolved." To a good medium, a haunted house presents no insoluble mystery. She can usually discover both the cause and the remedy. If property owners whose houses have been the scene of mysterious "disturbances" - and who sometimes lose tenants in consequence - realised how easily mediums might assist them, there would be fewer hauntings, more peace of mind among both the quick and the dead, and fewer fruitless probings in cellars, drains and garrets.

Helen Hughes, although she seldom undertakes such investigations, has succeeded in "laying" several ghosts in various parts of the country. In Scotland, she sometimes works for the Society for Recording Abnormal Happenings (under the auspices of the Edinburgh Psychic College, 30, Heriot Row). The report of the Society for 1943-44 contained the following account of how she brought peace and quiet to a disturbed household:

"In connection with the apparition and other manifestations in a house on the South Side of Edinburgh ... the householder (referred to as Mr. X) received us at the front door and showed us into the sitting room, where we met Mrs. X, who is in rather poor health.

"Mrs. Hughes stated that immediately on entering the house she had seen clairvoyantly two figures, the mother and sister of Mrs. X, who had informed her that they were responsible for the manifestations and that they were concerned about Mrs. X's health. They were frequently in the house with the aim of trying to help her, and the sister had tried to communicate by speaking and by other means.

"Mrs. X stated that only a week before she had heard sounds in the house as if someone was making an effort to speak. "Mrs. Hughes gave the name Emma, and also said that Mrs. X was just a duplicate of her mother. Mrs. X states she was aware of this. Mrs. Hughes volunteered that a prematurely born child was on the Other Side, so that Mr. and Mrs. X had two children there.

"Mrs. Hughes continued: 'You have a beautiful son. I can see him putting his arms round you. Did you cut a bit off his hair? (Mrs. X said this was correct.) He remembers it, though he was just a child.'

"Mrs. Hughes then went into trance and was controlled by her usual guide, who said: 'You are surrounded by many happy souls. You will continue to be helped from their side, particularly by your sister.'

"Thereafter Mrs. Hughes under control of her Indian child guide gave a number of names and related other facts connected with children and friends of the householder and his wife, who had passed over."

Mr. X wrote later: "Altogether it was a remarkable experience that we shall never forget. We have not heard one sound since your visit, and my wife has brightened up considerably."

Though Helen Hughes is interested in the more abstruse Chases of her mediumship, there are some questions which she never heard satisfactorily answered.

"How much there is to learn and understand!" she once commented. "How I wish with all my heart that more scientists would work at it!

"Why, for instance, when demonstrating on a platform, do I take one, two or three paces to the right or left, so that I can hear plainly what is being said to me? The improvement is instantaneous, but I do not understand the reason. Is there a different 'wave-length' one pace away? And must I move to 'tune in' with it?

"None of us here can afford to be dogmatic as to what actually happens in mediumistic manifestations, for even the spirit people once told my friends that with all their experience they are still puzzled over many things. It is a case of spirit people, by spirit magnetism, using a human organism to tell the world *there is no death.*

"Are we back at an age of miracles? With all my force let me say, 'There are no miracles.' I am merely demonstrating a law that has not yet been fully studied or defined."

Mrs. Hughes is fully alive to the deeply spiritual aspects of her great gift. "Spirit communicators," she says, "tell us the fact that there is no death is just the starting-off point of the message of the spirit world, for they want to see a regenerated earth, a world of beauty and happiness. They desire to free men from the materialism that keeps them in bondage.

"Very few non-Spiritualists seem to realise that it is not only people on this side who are desirous of hearing messages from the spirit world - the spirits are even more keen than ourselves. I did not seek the spirit friends; they sought me. Our only drawback is that there are not enough mediums to go round.

"Spiritualism to me and my fellow-mediums is not merely something interesting in the material way, but something which we hold most dearly and sacredly. It is the one thing we live for, and we feel that we are doing a great service not merely to mortals but also to the anxious spirits in allowing them to have communication with one another."

HELEN HUGHES

CHAPTER VI
ASTOUNDING PROOFS IN PUBLIC

Glendower: "I can call spirits from the vasty deep."
Hotspur: "Why, so can I, or so can any man. But will they come when you do call for them?"

Shakespeare, "Henry IV."

"But Lord! to see the absurd nature of Englishmen, that cannot forbear laughing and jeering at everything that looks strange."

Pepys, Diary.

Proof of powers of mental mediumship lies largely in two factors - the accuracy of the facts imparted and the impossibility of their laving been acquired by normal means. Helen Hughes's messages are characterised by an astonishing degree of something almost approaching omniscience.

Thousands of her listeners have been convinced of Survival by receiving messages themselves or by hearing those delivered to others. But as most messages are far more interesting and convincing to the receiver than to other listeners, I am reproducing in this chapter only a few typical examples. Repetition of case after case would become tedious.

One of the most remarkable features of her mediumship as mentioned in the previous chapter - is the fact that, under trance control, she speaks fluently in languages of which she has no knowledge whatever. Sceptics can neither deny the facts nor explain them away.

Reporting a meeting at St. Andrew's Hall, Glasgow, in September, 1937, "Psychic News" said: "In nearly every instance, Mrs. Hughes gave the full names of the spirit communicators and of their friends or relatives in the audience. "These included foreign names, in one case French and in another Swedish."

This is how Helen Hughes herself, in the "Sunday Sun," September 12, 1937, described one of the most notable of the occasions upon which she demonstrated this faculty of "speaking in tongues":

"In one of my trances I received a message from the other world. The sender was a young Portuguese who had passed over not very long before. He happened to leave this world while he was in his sick bed listening-in to a broadcast commentary of a fight in which one of the boxers was Tommy Farr.

"This exciting episode must have been carried by his intellect into the other world, as he told his mother, through me, of course - in perfect Portuguese - that he was keenly looking forward to witnessing the Farr-Louis world-title fight.

"He even had an opinion about the outcome of the fight and spoke rather pessimistically about his premonition that Tommy Farr would not manage to win the contest.

"This is the most interesting feature of many of my messages, which should surely satisfy even the most sceptical. Time after time I have received and transferred messages from the Other Side to people of different nationalities, though it is well known that I am not a linguist.

"My only language is my mother tongue. How could it be otherwise when my husband has been a miner all his days?"

It is difficult to select "typical" messages. Each one differs in context, character and evidential value. The following, however, delivered at a meeting in the Philosophical Hall, Leeds, on March 29, 1939, may be taken as "every-day" examples.

Helen Hughes: "First to a lady on the end of the row, with her hand to her mouth. You have someone named Alfred in the home. I get the message from your husband who is in spirit. He brings Lavinia, who is your mother; are you Nellie?" - "No, that's my sister."

"Well, she is talking about Nellie. There is someone belonging to you who was drowned, and a number of people think it was a case of suicide. I want to tell you it was not suicide, although he was drowned in a few inches of water."

Pointing to another woman: "Is your name Nellie?" - "Yes." "Well, then, you knew Mr. Bramwell, and I have to tell you that Mr. Bramwell is here and has brought Harry and Mrs. Wilson. She says she's all right now, and thanks you for what you did for her. She suffered from a weak heart. She tells me your name is Boynton.' - "Correct."

At a meeting at Gateshead on September 27, 1936: "There is a young woman here named Eva, who was a musician." This was claimed by two people. Singling out one of them, she said: "You are Eva's mother. She played the piano, and she had a companion, Elsie, who also has passed over. Her full name is Eva Huxley. I get the name Margaret Murritt, and she is calling out 'Fragile'. She shows me a hamper with puppies in it. She says she is Maggie, and when she was a baby you put her in the hamper and called her fragile, and the name stuck to her for some time. Is that so?" - "Yes."

"She tells me that you have been to the cemetery today, and she was with you when you stood at the grave and wept. She says you are not to do it. You have heard knockings in the house and you have several times got out of bed and gone to look for them. They have made you nervous. You have nothing to fear; it is your daughter knocking.

"There is a Mrs. Richardson in the gallery. I get the name Jimmie Richardson. I have to tell you that he was very far from Spiritualism when he was on earth. It would have been very strange to him. He has brought William Clark with him. Clark was a rough diamond, and Jimmie often saved him from trouble. Jimmie worked in an office by himself, and he often hid Clark in his office when he had a little to drink, and saved a lot of trouble.

"Jimmie Richardson brings Robert and Lizzie, and also Mary Bewick. He tells me your godmother was Mary McIntyre, and she was in some way connected with an off-licence for the sale of beer, when you were fourteen to seventeen years of age." - "Quite right!" (Note that seven correct names were given in one message.)

"There is a Mrs. Bell, called Grannie Bell, who comes for someone named Margaret. She was beloved in her neighbourhood. Whenever there was sickness or babies she was there. She brings with her Mary Elizabeth Bagster. She also brings your sisters Alice and Mary Blair. She tells me that when you were young you had a kick from a horse, or someone did, and she helped to treat them." - "Correct."

Many times during the war, Helen Hughes was able to relieve the terrible anxiety of parents by revealing that their missing sons had not been killed but were prisoners of war. Not once was she wrong. This is how she described one of these incidents to me:

"Before me was a woman in deepest mourning. Her son, first reported missing, she had now received news, had been killed.

"I was conscious that standing beside me was the father of this poor woman. He had passed on many years ago. He begged me to assure his daughter that her son had not been lolled, but was a prisoner - and that she would have confirmation of this in a few days. I passed on the message.

"'Oh!' exclaimed the mother, 'if I could only believe it!' But it was all true, and a letter from the War Office confirmed the joyful news soon after."

At a demonstration at the Caxton Hall, London, in May, 1938, there was an unusual incident. Helen Hughes broke off one message to repeat the word "cobwebs." The recipient of the message at once acknowledged that it was the name of his house!

At a meeting at Doncaster in February, 1937, Mrs. Hughes asked: "Is there anyone who worked in a pickling factory? There is a woman here with an apron on, and such a strong smell of onions."

A woman in the audience raised her hand, and Mrs. Hughes continued: "This woman now shows me some bottles of onions and tells me her name is Meg, and she worked beside you at this factory. She says it is not usual for workwomen to go to work with umbrellas, but she did, because, on returning home, she used to fill it with onions, and you knew it. Is this correct? Meg Simpson wants to know." The woman acknowledged that the message was correct in every particular.

I should like at this point to quote from the "Sunday Sun" part of the report of my friend "Maxwell Scott" of his private sitting with Helen Hughes - not because it is any more remarkable than most of her cases, but because it is the personal record of a trained observer.

After giving him the name of his father and describing how he died, Helen Hughes said:

"The other John is called John Wilson, but you would know him as Jack. For recognition he brings a great cloud of chloroform - so strong that you should be able to smell it.

"He holds out his arm and smiles and says, 'they made a pin-cushion of me, but it's all right now.' He points to his hip. That last operation was too severe and did no good. He says: 'We're all here, and of course we're not dead. Great revelations are coming soon.' With him he brings William Wilson."

Of this message, "Maxwell Scott" wrote: "Jack Wilson was the name of a young man who, some years ago, lay in the next bed to me in hospital for fifteen months. One year in those circumstances is equal to twenty years of a normal friendship. In the last few years of his life he had thirty-three operations. The last was on his hip, and I know it to be a fact that it was largely an experiment, and that the ward sister afterwards remonstrated with the young surgeon because of its severity. Wilson never looked like making any recovery after it.

"The message, 'We're all here,' has a meaning for me. In addition to Jack Wilson, eleven more of my hospital friends died. I did not know any William Wilson....

"Back to Newcastle I went - to a street in the West End, to seek the mother of Jack Wilson. I explained to her about the séance and the messages I had received.

"'Now,' I said, 'did you know anyone called William Wilson?

"'Yes,' she told me, 'William was Jack's twin brother, who died shortly after birth.'"

Here is the story of one of her wartime messages of consolation, as Mrs. Hughes related it herself

"One day a young wing-commander was sent to me. His brother, also an airman, had recently crashed. His mother was broken up, and to try to find some consolation for her he thought, rather sceptically, he would 'see if there was anything in this talk of another world.'

"He came out of his interview with me with an entirely new view - point of life. 'I know now,' he said, 'what I never realised before, that there genuinely is another world - a spiritual world - besides this one.'

"I had 'tuned in' to his father, who had died two years previously, and who poured out eagerly evidence of his brother, technical details of the 'crash,' and family news which the son could only confirm on appealing to his mother - a crowd of information showing how he, the father, was following closely the life and work of this wing-commander.

"I could give you hundreds of cases of this type."

There was a striking incident at the Edinburgh Psychic College when Mrs. Hughes dictated to a woman sitter a number, running into six figures, which she said was printed on a ticket *in a drawer at the sitter's home.* The woman took a note of the number, and subsequently confirmed that it was correct. On another occasion at the College, Mrs. Hughes gave the number of a crashed aeroplane - 127.

A particularly evidential message was given by Mrs. Hughes at a meeting in Glasgow. She told a sitter - who acknowledged the correctness of the fact - that he was born with a caul, still in the family's possession.

There was another impressive incident at the same meeting. At the morning session, Mrs. Hughes had given one very evidential message, but not the full name of the communicator. She said that he belonged to Crown Street, Aberdeen, explained that he had fallen over a cliff while on holiday, referred to another address, to his office, and the name of an associate, McKenzie, and gave a message for his wife.

At the evening meeting, he manifested again. Helen Hughes repeated his remark: "You did not give my name correctly this morning. I said only half what I wanted to say. My name is Duncan Davidson Campbell."

One of the most evidential, though at first sight trivial, messages ever given by Mrs. Hughes was at the Edinburgh College in December, 1944.

Pointing to a woman in the audience, she exclaimed, "Madam, are you wearing your husband's hat?"

The question seemed such an improbable one that even Helen Hughes - who had, of course, heard it repeated to her clairaudiently - paused almost incredulously, remarking, "I don't know whether I can ask that question, it sounds so impossible. All right. . ."

The woman in question immediately agreed that she was wearing her husband's hat. It was a red Army beret which, with the addition of a suitable decoration; made quite a becoming headgear. Helen Hughes told her, in addition, that her husband had been wounded in the left arm, and added further details.

Obviously struck by the unusual circumstances, the medium then asked the sitter whether it was possible for her to have had any prior knowledge of these facts, as critics had often alleged that there was collusion between her and recipients of messages. The woman volunteered that Mrs. Hughes had no knowledge of her whatever.

If such evidence as this is trivial, then all evidence is trivial. Despite countless similar proofs of the unseen powers which guide our destinies, several local clergymen - Helen Hughes mentioned at the same meeting - had recently been fulminating against the College, declaring that it should be closed down. On the other hand, several more enlightened local clergymen are regular speakers at the College.

HELEN HUGHES 1963

CHAPTER VII
THE TRAP THAT FAILED

"No man's knowledge can go beyond his experience."
Locke, "Essay on the Human Understanding."

Sitters who regard the medium as a kind of magician who can be left to do all the work and provide all the proof, without any effort on their part, are as unreasonable as if they expected her to conduct a one - sided telephone conversation with them. It takes two to make a message, as it does to make a quarrel. The medium, of course, plays the principal role, but the sitter should at least be intelligently responsive.

Sitters seldom realise how much depends on them as well as on the medium. Animosity is inimical, and an open mind conducive, to the best results. The attitude of the sitter should be unprejudiced, friendly if possible, receptive and attentive. A sympathetic atmosphere helps the medium, and a hostile atmosphere hinders her, in much the same way as it affects an actor on the stage. Most people, even without being psychic, can feel these two extremes, if they exist to any marked degree, upon entering a room.

The attitude of sitters ranges from the actively antagonistic, or sceptical, to the friendly and sympathetic, and even to the unintelligent and the too-eagerly-credulous. Those at both ends of this scale are bad sitters.

The emanations of the hostile mind often destroy all possibility of the very evidence which might convince it, and the bigot remains a bigot still. The unintelligent sitter, whose memory and association of ideas are faulty, lets the medium down by failing to acknowledge facts; the over-eager sitter sometimes leads the medium temporarily astray by 'jumping in" to acknowledge a message intended for some other sitter.

This eagerness is understandable. In a large audience it is obvious that only a small percentage can receive messages, and the disappointment of some of the sitters is often pathetic. There is disappointment, we are assured, on the Other Side as well. The medium does what she can - but there are not enough mediums.

It should be stressed that the sitter need not necessarily believe in the medium to obtain good results. The sitter can be critical, even sceptical, of the medium's powers, without having an unduly adverse effect on her, providing he preserves an equable frame of mind. On this point Helen Hughes once wrote:

"Recipients of messages play an important part. If they speak up loudly they create a vibration which assists the medium. It also encourages the spirit communicator, who can hear the voice of the person he is trying to reach.

"It is much the same at a voice séance - people who speak up help the conditions. Applause has a séance - effect.

"A cold and unsympathetic person defeats his own purpose by closing the avenues he seeks to explore. Yet I can recall occasions when my demonstrations have been at their best in. what appeared to be most uncongenial conditions. Scepticism and opposition sometimes call forth an additional effort from the spirit friends. But demonstrating in uncongenial conditions leaves me feeling more tired than usual, as though an extra strain had been made on my energies."

It must also be emphasised that the advantage of a sympathetic atmosphere does not in any sense imply the need for material assistance in the form of hints or prompting by the sitters. Their part is passive, and their stimulus to the medium almost entirely mental. Good mediums prefer sitters to reply briefly to points, not to begin making statements. A "Yes" or a "No," or "That is correct," is usually sufficient. The medium does most of the talking, but there are no leading questions. Sitters should speak up clearly and promptly if they think a message applies to them, or if any item is incorrect.

Good mediums as a rule like to work among strangers, as this rules out the oft - repeated but ridiculous allegation that they deliver messages only to people they know. Helen Hughes often arrives at a hall containing thousands of strangers, only a few minutes before the meeting, sees none of them beforehand, and yet gives messages to many so far back as clearly to be unrecognisable from the platform. These sitters often testify emphatically that they have never seen the medium before.

Some newspaper cuttings describing Helen Hughes's demonstrations record how jeering interrupters were silenced by the messages she gave them. "Frequently," says one such account, "Mrs. Hughes asked, 'Do you know me? Is there any way in which I could have known these things?' Always the answer was 'No.'"

Some sitters are inclined to be selfish, and attempt to keep the medium in conversation. One such sitter played a shabby trick - though not at a demonstration by Mrs. Hughes - as was evidenced by a whispered remark to a friend, "I find that by pretending not to know who the medium is referring to, I get a longer message."

Incidentally, for the benefit of those who believe they have "a better chance at the front," it may be mentioned that this makes no difference. They may be fortunate, but the medium is as likely to point out anyone else in the hall as those in the front seats. This is not of her choosing; she delivers the messages as she receives them.

It is perhaps at private sittings that Helen Hughes comes more closely in contact with the idiosyncrasies of sitters.

Some sitters consider mediums fair game, and set out to trap them if they can. Needless to say, no sitter has ever succeeded in "trapping" Helen Hughes - though several have been "caught" themselves.

A common practice is to give false names - a subterfuge which she always detects. Perhaps this form of deception is justified as a test, or to provide against possible publicity, but it is inconsistent of sitters, ready and eager to expose mediums for "fraud," to resort themselves to cheating without scruple.

When sitters fail in endeavouring to trap mediums, they seldom have the grace to apologise. In one exceptional case, the sitter made amends handsomely for his unjustifiable suspicion. Attending a group séance, he used a false name, but when Mrs. Hughes came over to him she said: "Your wife is here. She says, 'When did you change your name? When I married you, you were called So-and-so.'"

Helen Hughes gave him additional family evidence. Later he told her that if she had given him evidence bearing on the false name he would have prosecuted her. Instead, at his own expense, he inserted an advertisement in a local newspaper declaring his faith in her mediumship.

The medium scored similarly on another occasion, as related by Mr. O. J. Wendlandt in the "Sheffield Telegraph."

"I am reminded," he wrote, "of a Sheffield business man who, having had a remarkable sitting with Mrs. Helen Hughes, one of our best mediums, was so impressed that, when she came again, he telephoned asking if he might bring two ladies to see her.

"He introduced one as Mrs. Blank and the other as his wife. As soon as the medium was in trance the control said to the first lady, 'You are not Mrs. Blank,' and to the other, 'You are not Mrs. _____' (the wife). This was quite correct, as he had purposely transposed the ladies and their names. I know this to be a true incident."

Only rarely does the medium encounter what might be termed the methodical or "scientific sitter," who takes careful notes of the proceedings.

Three such records of private sittings are among my material. They are detailed typewritten accounts, of considerable interest, and further particulars will be found in another chapter. In passing, however, it may be mentioned, with regard to one of the sittings, that some additional notes, by an independent commentator, stress that the medium knew nothing about the investigator, and add, "In all Spiritualists' National Union churches the medium is never told the name of the sitter."

Remarking on the fact that the medium gave the name of the sitter's wife correctly as Jean Anderson Blackburn, the commentator also wrote: "The chances against a correct guess must be millions to one. . . . The whole sitting was simple, straightforward and without a flaw."

When Helen Hughes demonstrated at the meetings arranged by the London Spiritualist Alliance at the Caxton Hall, Westminster, and Folkestone Town Hall in 1936, full shorthand notes were taken and typewritten transcripts sent to as many of the recipients of messages as supplied their names and addresses, with a request that they would comment on the correctness or inaccuracies - of the information given to them. This request was complied with in a considerable proportion of the cases.

Of eight persons who received messages at the Caxton Hall meeting, six said they had never previously sat with Mrs. Hughes; the other two had been at one of her public meetings. Almost every report sent in referred to "very good" or "excellent" evidence.

At a Folkestone meeting, Mrs. Hughes gave messages to fourteen people, of whom eleven sent in reports. The number would probably have been larger but for an unfortunate misunderstanding. At the opening of the meeting the chairman announced that copies of the shorthand notes of messages - meaning, of course, transcribed copies - would be sent to those who gave their names and addresses. Certain members of the audience were heard to remark that copies of the report would be useless to them, as they "could not read shorthand."

Many of those who did write, however, expressed appreciation for the messages, and said they had never before sat with Mrs. Hughes.

Five or six names were given to and recognised by one sitter, and detailed confirmation of messages was sent by several others.

A similar experiment was made at a Caxton Hall meeting in October, 1938. One report presented interesting features. Mr. and Mrs. Maude, of Grange Park, N.21, reported that they had not sat privately with Mrs. Hughes, and did not know her personally, nor did any of their friends or relations know her. They had attended three of Mrs. Hughes's public meetings, and three times the same group of spirit friends had been described to them, with additional details on each occasion.

A pointed commentary by Dr. F. H. Wood on the reactions and shortcomings of certain sitters at a public meeting arranged by the Bradford Society for Psychical Research - but applying with equal force to other meetings - appeared in "Psychic News" on February 27, 1937.

Dr. Wood suggested that many sitters to whom descriptions were given badly needed coaching in the proper way to acknowledge them.

"Sometimes," he said, "these were received in utter silence, accompanied by a vague nod, easy enough to see from the platform but not by others in the audience.

"All recipients of these favours should acknowledge them by something more than a grudging nod to the medium who gives them so generously. Otherwise, time and mediumistic power are wasted."

Owing to lack of courtesy, he added, many in the audience who had no doubt hoped to receive messages went away disappointed, and not even comforted by the knowledge that what had been given to others was correct.

He suggested that printed programmes might be used to ask recipients to acknowledge a correct description or name, immediately and audibly.

More than once Mrs. Hughes had been obliged to force a corroboration which should have been given readily and spontaneously.

At this meeting Mrs. Hughes gave forty-one names, all identified by members of the audience.

With regard to the people who visit Spiritualist meetings with the sole object of detecting collusion, I wonder if they ever reflect that - even if it were physically possible - the cost of such collusion would be prohibitive. It would certainly greatly exceed the modest fee which the medium receives.

Critics have never been able to challenge Helen Hughes. Spiritualists can safely challenge the critics to detect any flaw in her remarkable mediumship.

CHAPTER VIII
ONE OF "THE FEW" RETURNS

> "All creeds I view with toleration thorough,
> And have a horror of regarding Heaven
> As anybody's rotten borough."
>
> Thomas Hood.

> "My idea of Heaven is that there is no melodrama in it at all; that it is wholly real." - Emerson.

Some of the evidence given by Helen Hughes, especially at private sittings, is so remarkable as to deserve a separate chapter. The incidents here recounted constitute more than mere "messages." They are true life stories - gripping moments from the drama of life triumphant over death in which medium and sitters play their parts.

Most messages are necessarily brief, and completely understood only by the sitters concerned. In this chapter, the background is revealed of some outstanding cases, whose evidence for Survival is compelling.

The salient story is that of the contact established by Mrs. 'Hughes with some of the heroes who fell in the Battle of Britain. Several of these gallant lads beyond the bourne from which travellers *do* return have spoken to their parents through Mrs. Hughes. Air Chief Marshal Lord Dowding, who commanded Britain's fighters during the historic battle, has dedicated the remainder of his retired life to the championship of another cause, no less historic - the cause of Spiritualism. That immortal motto "Per ardua ad astra," has an even deeper significance for him now.

Lord Dowding has studied Spiritualism intensively. He has investigated the powers of several mediums, including Helen Hughes, and has spoken on the same platform with them more than once.

At a meeting in St. Andrew's Hall, Glasgow, in May, 1944, he averred that it was no longer necessary to prove

Survival. "It has been proved over and over again ad nauseam," he declared.

The story of the return of one in particular of these deathless airmen is of absorbing interest. He was Pilot-Officer Douglas W. Hogg, the only son of a Scottish business man, Mr. Thomas Hogg, of Rouken Glen Road, Thorniebank, Glasgow. The parents of Douglas Hogg are convinced that he has returned to them several times, and that death after all is only a temporary separation. Helen Hughes was able to raise - these bereaved parents from the depths of despair to the supreme consolation of reunion.

Douglas, like many other young men, was attracted by flying, and joined the R.A.F.V.R. in 1937. He was shot down, at the age of twenty-three, on September 3, 1940 - just a year after Britain's declaration of war against Germany. Before his plane was hit, he and his gunner had destroyed or damaged five German machines. A moment before he died, he called out to the gunner, "Bale out, they've got me." Those were his last earthly words.

His parents were desolate. Nothing could console or interest them. One evening, however, not long after their bereavement, Mr. Hogg remembered a conversation some years before with a friend, a hard-headed business man, who claimed to have had many communications from the spirit world.

Mr. Hogg knew very little about Spiritualism, beyond a few books he had read in his early youth. Fortunately he possessed an open mind. He knew his friend to be a practical man, and to have studied psychic phenomena thorough for several years, and decided to get in touch with him again.

In the meantime, he met another business friend who, after expressing deep regret at the death of Douglas, asked the surprising question, "What would you say if I told you that I spoke to Douglas a few nights ago?"

Mr. Hogg was at first dumbfounded, but, remembering his other friend, replied, "I would believe you."

He, accompanied this friend to a group séance a few nights later, but, though he received some evidence, did not regard it as overwhelmingly convincing. He decided to have a private sitting in company with his friend the following week.

At this sitting, he received what he acknowledged to be "substantial evidence," but he still had some misgivings because his friend could conceivably have imparted some of his family history to the medium.

He then visited the first friend, who advised him to watch the Press announcements of Spiritualist meetings for the name of Helen Hughes. He warned Mr. Hogg not to communicate his intention to anybody, but merely to arrange for a sitting.

Early in November that same year, Mr. Hogg saw an announcement in the "Glasgow Herald" that Helen Hughes was to address meetings in the St. Vincent Street Church, headquarters of the Glasgow Association of Spiritualists.

He attended one of the meetings, accompanied by his two daughters, was greatly impressed by Helen Hughes's demonstration, and arranged a sitting for the following evening. He and his two daughters, with his son-in-law, were welcomed by Mrs. Hughes, who knew nothing of their identity.

Within a few moments she announced the spirit presence of a young airman. "You are his dad," she said, turning to Mr. Hogg. Then, to his son-in-law, she said, "This boy calls you Ian, and passes his fingers through your hair as if to push your head back."

This was striking evidence for the family. Douglas had a playful and affectionate habit, whenever he entered a room where Ian was sitting, of running his fingers through Ian's curly hair.

Even more convincing evidence followed. "He calls himself Douglas," said Helen Hughes. Turning to the two girls, she said, "You are his sisters Isobel and Mary."

Helen Hughes then became entranced, and after a time Douglas himself was able to "take control."

Mr. Hogg afterwards said of the incident: "His conversational characteristics, apart from information concerning other relatives who had passed on, left no doubt in our minds as to his identity.

"By the end of the sitting each of us had the most convincing proof that it was Douglas who had returned. His mannerisms, the correctness of his information and his replies to questions clinched the matter beyond all shadow of doubt."

When Mr. Hogg suggested that Ian should ask Douglas a question, he propounded a difficult one. "Douglas," he said, "can you tell me the name of the plane you flew up from Ipswich for me about a year before the war?" Back came the answer like a shot, "You are pulling my leg now; it was the old Prague."

Helen Hughes visited the Hoggs at their home two months later, and again gave the family striking evidence of the presence of Douglas.

"Douglas is speaking about a set of gold cuff-links," she said. "He says they are in a drawer in his dressing-table. He is anxious that the ends should be mounted as rings and given to members of the family."

The family had no knowledge of the existence of the cuff-links, but one of the daughters, on searching, found them in a small case in the drawer. They ascertained later that the links were a prize which Douglas had won while on a cruise.

Douglas has returned to his parents several times since then, and through them has comforted numerous other bereaved people. He has "brought through" members of the Air Force and the other services who have given their names and addresses and other details, to be passed on to their families.

"We have been successful in tracing many of these people," reveals Mr. Hogg. "Most of them have accepted the fact of spirit return and have invariably written to express the great mental and spiritual uplift that accompanies the knowledge that their boys are not dead."

Mrs. Hogg is equally emphatic. "You can well appreciate what this revelation meant to me," she declares in a message to other bereaved mothers. "I am fully convinced of the happiness of our ultimate reunion.   Spiritualism has offered me irrefutable proof of Survival. What before was a belief is now a certainty. Now I understand that so-called death is but temporary separation. In Spiritualism there is a philosophy of profound interest based on facts which are gradually becoming indisputable."

At a meeting in the Usher Hall, Edinburgh, in May, 1944, Helen Hughes established "liaison" between Lord Dowding and a "dead" airman who once served under him. "Billy Cox, another airman, is standing here," she told a man in the audience. "He has just taken the salute to you," she observed, turning to Lord Dowding, who had addressed the meeting. "He says, 'The Chief's here.'"

A clergyman paid a tribute to the mediumship of Helen Hughes, and to the truth of Spiritualism, at a meeting in the Kingsway Hall, West Central London, in May, 1944. He was the Rev. George Sharp, a Sheffield Free Church minister, making his debut in London.

He explained that he was present in fulfilment of a pledge to her when she proved Survival to him through her mediumship. His interest is Spiritualism was first aroused after having conducted the funeral service of a member of his church. The dead man's wife called on him not long afterwards, the picture of radiant happiness, and declared that her husband had come back and spoken to her.

The Rev. Sharp and his wife concluded that she had gone mad, but, impressed by her obvious sincerity, he decided to investigate the subject himself.

His first "séance," purporting to be a transfiguration, was a farce, and he telephoned the secretary of a local Spiritualist society to say so. To his surprise she agreed with him, but invited him to attend a real séance. Later, he arranged a sitting with Helen Hughes. He and his wife were completely convinced.

"Things were told which were irrefutable," he said. "'There was no escape. I had spoken to the dead."

He concluded by revealing that he was speaking up and down the country, not only at propaganda meetings for Spiritualism but in orthodox churches, spreading the truth of Survival to fulfil his pledge.

A vivid account of a meeting with Helen Hughes, and of the extremely evidential messages she received from her, was given by Miss Esson Maule, a member of a well-known Scottish family, in the "People's Journal," November 28, 1936. The story is of exceptional interest on account of the prediction which Mrs. Hughes made to this sitter, and which, although it was at first rejected, and then forgotten, was eventually fulfilled to the letter. This was one of the comparatively rare occasions on which Mrs. Hughes has uttered predictions, and certainly one of the most noteworthy.

Miss Maule had studied psychic matters closely, had visited many mediums, and had herself possessed the gift of clairvoyance since her early years.

The sitting took place at Gayfield Square, Edinburgh, about three years before the account was first published. Miss Maule arranged it only twenty minutes before the meeting, which, so far as she was concerned, disposed of any suggestion that Mrs. Hughes knew the names of her sitters in advance.

Twelve people were present - none of them known to Miss Maule except the friend who brought her.

Mrs. Hughes told her that she saw a large red cross forming above her head. Miss Maule had done some first-aid training, but her chief interest at that time was in "hammering away for all I was worth trying to get the Government to move in the matter of laying down a scheme for those injured in road accidents."

"No one in the room, beyond my friend," she said, "could know about the work I was endeavouring to do as nothing had appeared in the newspapers at that time."

Then Mrs. Hughes described an old gentleman standing beside Miss Maule with his hand on her shoulder.

"He is calling you 'Little Jock,'" she said.

"I knew instantly by the description that she was describes my grandfather, John Maule," continued Miss Maule, "and when she added 'Little Jock' I knew she was absolutely correct, as that was the name he called me.

"As he died when I was eight you will realise that no one could have known that, and Mrs. Hughes was absolutely genuine in her clairvoyance. A moment later she looked upwards and said, 'He tells me your name is Maule.'"

Helen Hughes next told her that she expected to go to London soon, but that there would be a postponement. Miss Maule had arranged an interview with the Minister of Transport early in October, and intended going to London in a few days, but, as it turned out, the visit was postponed three times.

She told Miss Maule that while in London she would unexpectedly meet a man who had been her enemy for eighteen years. "But," added Mrs. Hughes, "you will become great friends until he dies." She described a man of outstanding personality.

Miss Maule assured her that she was entirely wrong, and that she knew no such man.

In the last week of October Miss Maule received an urgent message to travel to London at once. During her visit, she went to call on a friend. The friend was out, and she was shown into the drawing-room where she found a man also waiting. He possessed a delightful personality, and they had become fast friends by the time their hostess arrived.

It was not until they had finished tea that their hostess realised that they had not met before, and made a formal introduction. On hearing each other's names they stared in astonishment, and then both burst out laughing.

"Thus ended an acrimonious dispute of eighteen years' standing," wrote Miss Maule. "This gentleman, who was of high military rank, turned out to be the officer whom several of us held responsible for the withholding of certain privileges, credits and medals due to my first-aid corps.

"The dispute had gone on intermittently during the eighteen years, sometimes dying down for quite a long time and then bursting out again. I had never met him, and the dispute had been carried on by correspondence only. Just at the moment of meeting him for the first time the dispute had reached a particularly bitter stage as, owing to some technicality in the regulations, war medals were being withheld from some of the corps members who were entitled to them.

"Within a few minutes the original cause of the dispute was cleared up completely between us, as I was able to prove that certain orders which had been issued during wartime had never reached me.... We became very firm friends, and this friendship lasted until his death, which took place suddenly about a year after I first met him.

"Curiously, during all this time I quite forgot about Mrs. Helen Hughes's clairvoyant reading, which was so perfectly correct, and it was not until I returned to Edinburgh about a fortnight later that it suddenly recurred to my mind, and I realised that her description of my 'enemy of eighteen years' fitted exactly. Immediately I realised that everything she had told me had been correct I wrote and told her so."

Helen Hughes herself once related the following story, of an astonishingly evidential message.

"Two distraught parents came to me in Edinburgh for a trance sitting," she said. "I knew nothing of their trouble or history. During trance, their boy, who had passed out in hospital, spoke to them through me. He told them of his illness, proved his identity in the most intimate way, and then at the end of P's conversation mentioned that the surgeon had done his best to save him by injection, in a last attempt to resuscitate him.

"When I returned to normal, the parents said they were astounded at the evidence. It had been a glad family reunion, but they knew nothing about that last injection made by the surgeon. They made inquiries at the hospital, and were told by the matron in charge that no injections had been administered to their boy.

"This presented a flaw in the evidence that disconcerted the parents. But imagine their surprise and joy when later the surgeon spoke to them on the telephone and said he had made the injection in secret, and expressed a desire to meet 'this medium' who had told them something he thought no one knew but himself.

"The 'flaw' in the evidence proved to be of the greatest value in excluding telepathy as an explanation of the evidence they had received through me."

Most spirit messages are of an entirely personal nature, but occasionally they link up with national events - epic, dramatic or disastrous. A remarkable message; delivered by Helen Hughes at Holland Street, Glasgow, m June, 1939, convinced the sitters that she had established direct contact with a member of the crew of the ill - fated submarine Thetis.

One of the sitters was a Mr. Tate, attending with a materialist friend - Mr. Joseph Tedford - who brought two relatives with him. There were altogether twelve sitters.

Mr. Tate, describing the seance, said that Mrs. Hughes seemed unusually perturbed and puzzled. Turning to him she said: "There's something unusual here. . . . Do you know anyone connected with the sea, someone connected with the Navy? . . . Good gracious! The Thetis, yes, the Thetis submarine. There's someone here making an effort to come through. Watch carefully; the guides will have to come through and help."

She then gave signs of violent sickness. After an interval she went into trance, and displayed further symptoms of sickness. Mazeeta then took control and said to one of the sitters, a Mr. Kirk: "Come here, I want you to help a man from the Thetis. I want them here, and I will let Willie through."

The medium again began gasping and choking, and it was evident that another entity was taking control. Turning to Mr. Tate's friend the communicator addressed him by name, calling him Uncle, and said: "It was all due to a blocked valve; it's all right now, but pray for the men in the Thetis. God bless Captain Bolus (Lieut.-Commander G. H. Bolus. He did very well; it was a sacrifice. Pray for him."

Mr. Tate reported: "My materialist friend is uncle to one of the men who went down in the Thetis, a fact which was quite unknown either to the medium or sitters." Immediately afterwards, the Thetis visitant wrote down his name - William Orrock - through Mrs. Hughes, in his own handwriting.

Another account of the same sitting was written by James Watson, an official of the church, who stated that Joseph Tedford attended with a Mrs. Mary Rae, also a stranger to the medium.

Mrs. Rae and Tedford signed a statement declaring that through Helen Hughes they identified this Thetis victim who "communicated from the spirit world, gave his full name, and spoke to his uncle.

"Mr. Tedford was very doubtful about Spiritualism before the sitting," added Mr. Watson, "but he was fully convinced after receiving such wonderful proof."

To those unfamiliar with such phenomena, it may be explained, with reference to the "gasping and choking" of the medium, that the conditions immediately preceding death are frequently reproduced by spirit communicators "coming through" for the first time. These symptoms in the medium need occasion sitters no alarm, nor apprehension that the returning spirit is suffering; the phase is associated with the return to "earth conditions," and is only momentary.

One of her most dramatic and convincing messages - the fulfilment of a pact made before death - was delivered by Mrs. Hughes at the meeting in the Kingsway Hall, London, referred to earlier in this chapter.

"Please say Russia, Russia," suddenly exclaimed Mrs. Hughes to a woman in the audience, who immediately acknowledged that the word was evidential. After the meeting, the woman divulged the meaning of this enigmatic message.

Many years before, she said, Helen Hughes had visited her home in the Isle of Wight. She herself was convinced of Spiritualism, but her husband was a complete sceptic. After Helen Hughes had left, he concluded a discussion with his wife by saying that, if he should die first, he would come back through the medium and say the word "Russia," which he selected because he had travelled extensively in that country.

He did come back, and not only repeated the agreed "code" word, but gave his name and details of the circumstances in which he had died.

This meeting, too, was notable for an incident discountenancing the fallacy that the dead are called against their will. It demonstrated, once again, that the unseen host, who cannot possibly all communicate at one meeting, are as anxious to attract the medium's attention as the sitters. On this occasion, Helen Hughes broke of to say that a little girl, Barbara Davidson, had put her hand on her and pleaded for her message to be given.

"For half an hour," reported "Psychic News" of this meeting, "the gulf of death was ridged by living, warm, human contacts. The dead behaved naturally. There was no aura of glorified sanctity. They were human beings delighted at the opportunity of proving that their love was stronger than their death."

CHAPTER IX
THE "MYSTERY MAN" WAS CONVINCED

> "Not where the wheeling systems darken,
> And our benumbed conceiving soars!
> The drift of pinions, would we hearken,
> Beats at our own clay - shuttered doors.
>
> "The angels keep their ancient places;
> Turn but a stone, and start a wing!
> 'Tis ye, 'tis your estranged faces,
> That miss the many - splendoured thing."
> Francis Thompson.

This chapter deals with three conspicuous cases in which Helen Hughes gave bereaved parents indisputable proof of survival. These are among the most notable and convincing records of her mediumship, and are particularly valuable because of the detailed and emphatic statements, voluntarily written by the sitters, confirming the accuracy of the evidence. One of the parents was extraordinarily cautious and methodical in concealing his identity from the medium.

The evidence, in short, effectively counters two common criticisms - that mediumistic demonstrations do not constitute proof of Survival, and that bereaved persons are easily "hood-winked." The truth is that the bereaved, of all people, are the most exacting in their demands for the proof which, at the hands of such mediums as Helen Hughes, they invariably receive.

The cry of the incredulous - too apathetic and indolent to investigate the readily - accessible facts - always been: "Where is the proof? Show us it, and we will believe."

Spiritualists are not concerned in pursuing these inert armchair cavillers with pleadings and proofs. Mahomet must come to the mountain. The phrase, the ever-open door, was never more justified than in its application to Spiritualism. Those who misguidedly believe that Spiritualism is unintellectual, unconvincing, furtive, obscure or demoralising are closing the door in their own faces. Proof, abundant and overwhelming, is to be gained for the asking. No, it is not proof which is lacking, but the capacity for seeking and discerning it.

The important question is: What is proof? We cannot carry it about in our pockets. Descriptions of those compelling séance-room phenomena, which afford complete proof of Survival to all thinking men and women who have witnessed them, appear to the uninitiated to be the distorted imaginings of liars or of well-meaning dupes. Let the trained, observant investigator produce never so many verbatim notes, photographs, gramophone records, apports, etc., as well as independent witnesses, and the sceptic dismisses them all as inaccurate, faked or deluded.

Yet Spiritualism has piled proof upon proof, until its libraries groan in travail. Casual inquirers do not realise how the truth has been suppressed. It exists, in all its magnitude, and it is invincible, but it is waging war against the evils of intolerance.

Sceptics often imply, in effect, that the only way to prove Survival would be to produce spirits in a test-tube. They never ask theologians to perform the same miracle with angels. The proof is presented in the seance room; it cannot be carted about like a peep-show. It is as irrational, and as insulting to the integrity of the countless reputable people who have investigated the subject, to decry their findings on such a pretext as it would be, say, to dispute whether a returning theatre goer had seen a play because he could not produce the actors on the spot.

Samples of ectoplasm *have* been taken and analysed, but that, of course, does not convince the sceptics. Who can prove to them that it was taken from genuine materialisations? The focus of proof is in the place where it is demonstrated.

But - here is the interesting point - how is proof of facts assessed in other spheres of life? My dictionary defines proof as: "Test or trial; demonstration; convincing evidence."

Scientific proof, I suppose, consists of an exact demonstration that, under given conditions, certain results occur. It is a demonstration of cause and effect. Similarly, psychic research demonstrates that, under suitable conditions, certain phenomena occur. But whereas the results of scientific experiments are usually acknowledged as conclusive, those of psychical experiments are not.

Evidence of many matters is accepted as valid on far less substantial grounds than that on which Spiritualism is based. In everyday life it is not necessary or expedient for people to experience everything they believe. The man in the street accepts as a matter of course the assurances of the appropriate authorities as to a thousand-and-one scientific or commonplace facts. The proofs are available if he wishes to verify them.

The proper authorities upon Spiritualism are Spiritualists, but to what extent does the world accept their testimony? And what more conclusive proofs does it demand than those already afforded? The proofs are sufficient to convince all reasonable people. One can only conclude that most people are unreasoning.

The most significant aspect of this question of proof is the legal one. Many men have been hanged upon evidence far more frail and far less objective than the evidence for Survival adduced by a single séance.

In a court of law, the magistrates or the judge and jury do not see the murder, the burglary or the accident. They hear statements by witnesses, most of whom visited the scene after the event, or who were never there at all. The law does not demand the re-enaction of the occurrence. It requires only that the evidence shall be such as to leave no reasonable doubt, one way or the other, in the minds of the adjudicators.

The evidence, indeed, is often circumstantial, but points clearly in one direction, and the testimony of credible witnesses is accepted as proof because it pieces together. In the eyes of the law, an event may even be proved without anyone having witnessed it. Yet judicial proof is not *scientific* proof; it is not infallible, though in most cases it is reliable.

What happens when Spiritualist witnesses, all of whom were together at the material place and time, appear as actual eyewitnesses? Their evidence is flouted in court and ridiculed in the Press. But since mediums are incontinently condemned, not for fraud but for practising mediumship, it is scarcely likely that the evidence of Spiritualists will be accepted as proof of Survival, or of anything else, in court or out of it.

Take another example of proof, adequate in law. In an identification parade - I have participate in some, not under duress, but to oblige the police - the accused stands silently in line with a number of men of similar build. Witnesses are required to point him out, without prompting, as the man alleged, say, to have snatched a handbag. They may have seen him only once before in their lives, and only for a fleeting moment, but if they select him from a dozen or so strangers, the fact becomes part of the proof of the case.

When a witness of a materialisation seance describes how he recognised clearly not only the features but the voice and the intimate conversation of a loved one whom he had known all his life, he is disbelieved and derided. Surely it is an anomaly that Spiritualists generally are not acknowledged as authorities upon the subject which they have perhaps spent a lifetime in studying. The popular view is that they do not know what they are talking about.

The scientist, detached and systematic, demands scientific proof from the Spiritualist. If he is sufficiently enterprising, he secures the evidence himself. Many scientists have proclaimed their conviction of Survival, and others, cautiously, admit "a residuum which cannot be explained." They are obliged to admit, at the least, that the phenomena are indefinable by ordinary terms. Therein lies the chief difficulty of proof. As Mr. Horace Leaf, the well - known medium and lecturer, once remarked to me, "Proof is very elusive." The phenomena are transient. They cannot as a rule be retained for examination, except in recorded form. This, of course, applies in some degree to most evidence and to most experiments.

With delightful inconsistency, many of those who demand proof of Survival from Spiritualists profess themselves to believe in a variation of Survival - i.e., a deferred immortality. They maintain, not that the dead survive and can communicate with us in the living present, but that they he asleep until some mythical "Day of Judgment" - a conception as unsound as some of the Bible stories they interpret literally, but for which there is no scientific or historical proof whatever.

Survival - not immortality - has been proved time after time, by many types of psychic phenomena. The proof, through the mediumship of Mrs. Hughes, lies in the analysis of the evidence. Principally, it comprises proof of identity. The sitters are convinced by the mannerisms, phraseology, vocabulary, and even the gestures, of the communicator (under trance control), and by the wealth of facts imparted - always unfamiliar to the medium, and often unknown at the time to the sitters themselves. Even pet names, and family nicknames and abbreviations - highly evidential though seemingly trivial points - are given. Those who have sat with Helen Hughes know what proof of Survival means.

Among the calumnies levelled against those who accept such evidence is the threadbare favourite that only in times of stress and sudden bereavement like the war do people turn towards it, uncritically, for spurious comfort. It is true that innumerable mourners during the war derived from

Spiritualism the complete consolation which they vainly sought in the Churches. They were not consoled by theories and assurances, however, but by facts; and they were not merely consoled, but convinced. Spiritualism has comforted thousands - but its victories belong to peace as well as war.

Certain of the more enlightened clergy recognise these facts, and testify to them on Spiritualist platforms. Describing the Work of Helen Hughes as "a grand ministry of helpfulness," to quote but one instance, a Glasgow clergyman, the Rev. D. Mackay, declared at a meeting in the Edinburgh Psychic College that it had been the means of "convincing the doubting, cheering the desolated and comforting the broken - hearted." He added: "If that is not a divine mission what is it? It is a most God-like work."

At the same meeting, the Rev. G. G. Morgan, another local clergyman, characterised Mrs. Hughes as "one of the great seers of the world," and remarked that there were many broken-hearted people who could be comforted only by definite knowledge.

Critics often express surprise that agnostics are "converted" to Spiritualism - as though it were some form of religious mania! They deplore the step as an intellectual retrogression. Yet agnosticism is the most logical approach to Spiritualism, since it frees the mind from prejudices, and agnostics are better fitted to decide what proof is than orthodox thinkers. Survival is not necessarily a religion, but a demonstrable scientific fact. I remind my materialist friends that in one essential particular I have the advantage of them; I have investigated the facts and they have not. But proof may be demonstrated and yet disregarded. Remember how the persecutors of Galileo refused to look through his telescope for fear of being convinced of the truth! Spiritualism brings us closer to ultimate reality than can "all the saints and sages" who have discussed the problem so learnedly and for so long.

The following cases - all of which were published in "Psychic News," illustrate how several parents were completely convinced by, the proof Helen Hughes offered them. One hard-headed investigator took such elaborate precautions to ensure anonymity that the evidence was rendered doubly conclusive. The unusual circumstances of this particular case were brought to light by an article by Maurice Barbanell, then editor of "Psychic News" describing his strange encounter, while on a visit to Leeds, with a "Mystery Man" who, despite doubts which prompted him, for his own satisfaction, to construct a "watertight" test case, was eventually convinced in thirty seconds.

The whole fascinating story was revealed after the publication of this article, in which the editor described how he had received a telegram, signed "Mystery Man," stating, "Mrs. Hughes was quite right." This telegram, which referred to the report of a meeting at Leeds, was a striking tribute to her mediumship. Here is the first episode of the story, as the editor related it:

"When I was recently in Leeds, I met a Yorkshireman who has just begun a painstaking inquiry into Spiritualism. Because of the elaborate precautions he took to conceal his identity from everyone connected with the Leeds Psychic Research Society, he was known as the 'Mystery Man.'

"All I knew was that he was a business man, for when I met him he was accompanied by two secretaries.

"Helen Hughes told me of his extraordinary behaviour when he arrived for a seance. When he came into the room she asked him to take a seat. He said nothing. In fact during the whole seance he scarcely uttered a word. When it was over he left almost without breaking his silence.

"Afterwards, he showed her the copious notes he had made, taking the precaution to leave a blank where there was a mention of a name, district or any reference that might give a clue to his identity.

"At tea he volunteered that he was convinced of Spiritualism in thirty seconds. Something said through Helen Hughes in trance clinched the matter for him. 'If I did not believe in Spiritualism,' he said, 'then I could not believe in anything. The proof is overwhelming.'

"He was a typically shrewd, rugged Yorkshireman. You would have thought him hard as nails. But I saw another side of his nature at the public meeting I addressed that night organised by the Leeds Psychic Research Society.

"Helen Hughes gave his wife a spirit message, one that described the passing of their son. While the medium gave these proofs I noticed the tears rolled down his face.

"Every word Helen said in this connection was taken down in shorthand by one of the secretaries. After the meeting, the Yorkshireman came to me, saying that he noticed I had taken notes. Would I let him have a transcript of the message to his wife?

"'To save time,' I said, 'I will read my notes over to your secretary.' I did so. Our notes tallied.

"When I came to the words, 'Doctor Bradley,' part of the message given by Helen Hughes, the secretary involuntarily mentioned that this name was wrong. Her employer, standing by, rebuked her for making this admission.

"The incident made me smile and I later recounted it to Helen Hughes. The following morning the medium told me that she had been unable to sleep during the night. While tossing restlessly in her bed she heard the name 'Bradbury.'

"'That is the name I should have given, not Bradley,' she said. The mistake is excusable to a clairaudient who has to listen - in - and Helen, very ill on that night, was not at her best."

Not knowing how to send this information to the Yorkshireman, the editor mentioned the fact at the end of the report of the meeting in "Psychic News," ending with the words, "Perhaps the 'Mystery Man' will let me know if that is right."

His telegram, "Mrs. Hughes was quite right," was the reply

There was a most interesting sequel to the publication of this article, when the "Mystery Man" himself sent in a long account of his experiences with Helen Hughes and other mediums, and of how he was convinced of Survival within thirty seconds of meeting Mrs. Hughes. This was published in "Psychic News" on May 31, 1941, with the explanation that the writer was called "Mystery Man" because his identity had never been disclosed to the mediums who had given him his evidence for Survival.

"At a time when mourning stalks the land," added this preface, "his account is one more proof that Spiritualism alone can give true solace to the bereaved."

Here is the "Mystery Man's" own story:

"Since the editor has in some measure introduced me to readers of 'Psychic News,' I feel it is incumbent upon me to add a little to what he has written. He cannot, even if he wished, ask me to do this since he does not know who I am. He says I am referred to in Leeds as the Mystery Man. I planned it that way as only by remaining quite unknown could any evidence offered to me be convincing. But I feel now that it would be both ungrateful and churlish not to make some public acknowledgment of the saving grace vouchsafed to me through spiritual aid.

"My son was a super-edition of myself. It seems out of place to be talking of oneself, but to convey what I think I owe to Spiritualists and Spiritualism to say, it cannot well be avoided.

"I was always big physically, but my son was six feet one, and all muscle, as fine a specimen of an Englishman as it would be possible to meet. He took particular care of his body and was a fine swimmer, a fine oarsman, an outstanding motor driver, a good squash player - in fact, an all - round athlete. My son was absolutely fearless. He would drive his car at 106 miles an hour and thoroughly revel in his mastery of the machine.

"In England again after the debacle in France, his orderly said to me: 'I would go anywhere with him. He gives us confidence.' No man could gain higher tribute than that, nor could another pay it.

"The sergeants of his regiment paid tribute to him in those famous words, 'In memory of a gallant gentleman!' The highest tributes were also paid him by his Commanding Officer.

"In his career he was equally distinguished. He took his medical degrees with medals and honours and he would undoubtedly have made a fine surgeon - the career he had mapped out. The matron of his hospital, indicating how everybody there had liked him, said, 'He was a doctor with a way of his own.'

"When the war broke out his first thought was to join up and he became Medical Officer of an artillery regiment.

"He was all man.

"He lived twenty-five vital, purposeful years, and everybody loved him.

"He and I had been pals together. We swam together, went canoeing together, motored together, went shooting together, attended the same gymnasium. Our last holiday together was in Devon in 1938, and I well remember an exiled Russian count who was spending a holiday there, saying, 'It does one good to see a father and son such pals as you two.'

"And then the catastrophe.

"The direst and blackest that could overtake his mother and myself.

"December 1st, 1940.

"That date is for ever burned into our souls. The date that made our lives without purpose; vain; a mockery to us.

"His mother and I were desolated, heartbroken, and inconsolable. Our yearning for him was an unbearable anguish. "In a month my hair had turned white and my physical condition was rapidly deteriorating.

"The thought that tormented me most was embodied in a gnawing doubt of his continued existence.

"What if he had been extinguished for ever! My fine lad no more!

"This thought kept me in a continual frenzy, a continual panic. I felt that if I could get some evidence of his continued existence it would quiet us and do something to ease our pain.

"I had been to four Spiritualist meetings during my life. The first was an address by Vale Owen, the second an ordinary Sunday meeting, the third a demonstration by Mrs. Helen Hughes - though I had forgotten the name.

"The fourth was a transfiguration séance and was the only one that my son had attended with me. At this latter we were not very popular as we expressed the view, perhaps with vigour, that 'these people will believe anything.' Anyhow, I had no evidence which meant anything to me and though I had always attended with an open mind I was not impressed.

"I remembered saying of Mrs. Helen Hughes that it was a very good performance of something - but what, I didn't know.

"Anyhow I now determined to visit a medium. I remembered that at Mrs. Hughes's meeting, the chair was taken by a Unitarian minister whose name I knew and who, I had observed, was a Freemason. I thought to use the latter fact in my approach, but determined to keep unknown to him. I then found that he had removed to another town sixty miles away. That suited me better, but on the day I had determined to go and see him, the snow came and made it impossible. All I wanted to get from him was the name and address of a reliable medium in his locality who, like himself, would not know who I was; the further from my town the better. The snow, however, had made the project impossible.

"I then thought of another gentleman in this town who has contributed several letters to the Press on Spiritualistic subjects. So in desperation I rang him up. He does not know me, and I did not tell him who I was. I said that what I wanted was the name of a medium say 40 to 50 miles away.

This gentleman did not know of anyone, but his wife referred the "Mystery Man" to another friend, through whom, after various other telephone calls, he contacted the Leeds secretary, who arranged a sitting for him with Mrs. Hughes.

"When he asked my name," continued the writer, "I told him I preferred to remain anonymous. He said he understood, and booked the sitting - 'anonymous.'

"I drove to Leeds with my wife, left the car in the station yard behind the Queen's Hotel where we had lunch. I left the car behind so that its registration number could not give any clue as to my identity. I went alone to the sitting so that no inadvertence on my wife's part could disclose information. I have no doubt that many will think such elaborate precautions absurd, but they were necessary to me. I went on the tram car to Hyde Park (Leeds) and inquired my way to Morton House. Mrs. Campbell opened the door. I was a complete stranger to her and she to me. I have met her on a few occasions since. I referred to her as 'the little old lady' and what a lovely old girl she is - a credit to the religious system which produced her.

"I said I had come for an appointment. She said, 'With Mrs. Helen Hughes?' I assented. She showed me into a room. . . In a short time the little old lady came and said Mrs. Hughes was ready and led me out across a passage, opened the door of another room, and Mrs. Hughes was walking across the room to meet me.

"I have given you something of my background, and led you to my crucial moment so that you may be able to appreciate somewhat the effect of Mrs. Hughes's revelation upon me.

"As she led me to a settee Mrs. Hughes said: 'Oh, sir, a very strong influence has come into the room with you. A bright, tall, beautiful boy - yes - your son. What a wonderful boy! But he does smell of a hospital, chloroform or something. Anyhow it is a hospital smell.' And then, looking up and sideways, she said: 'No, no, Doctor - I know the smell is not connected with your accident. I know, Doctor, I know.

"'He says he had an accident which never ought to have been, and in a flash he was gone.'

"She went on - 'He says you have come a long way to meet him but you needn't have done so as he has never left you and has come in the car with you today.' And then aside 'Forty miles, you say, from R . . .' and I thought she was go" to say the name of a town beginning with 'R,' but she said, 'No, no, Doctor, I hear you - Sheffield.'

"The editor has referred, albeit kindly, to my unashamed tears. I cannot be ashamed of them since I cannot control them. They are born of an emotion I always feel in the presence of either Mrs. Helen Hughes or Mrs. Susie Hughes *(These two mediums are not related to one another)*. When either is present I can feel my lad with an almost physical appreciation of his presence. I know he is alongside me.

"At the public meeting attended by the editor and referred to by him, the hall seemed full of him. It seemed solid with him and I knew long before what happened that he would compel Mrs. Hughes to bring a message from him to us.

"To come back to my sitting with Mrs. Helen Hughes. The remainder of the evidence was even more wonderful, but of such a personal and intimate nature as to prevent my telling it publicly. I might perhaps refer to an incident. She said, 'He's getting excited about an intimate belonging in your inside pocket.' I emptied my inside coat pocket and beyond a driving licence, identity card, insurance certificate, there was nothing, and I said so. But she said, 'Yes, he insists.'

"I then thought of my overcoat lying on the couch beside me and felt in the inside pocket, and brought out a dirty silk handkerchief. I will only say about this handkerchief that it is sacred to me. All the money in the world would not buy it, and the incident is overwhelming proof of Mrs. Hughes s direct communication with my lad.

The remainder of the "Mystery Man's" first narrative deals with subsequent sit ' s which he arranged, strictly anonymously, with other mums - Mrs. Susie Hughes, Mrs. Duncan, and Mrs. Bullock - which need not be described here, as they have only an indirect bearing on the evidence given by Helen Hughes. Referring to the evidence as a whole, however, he states:

"We are convinced that our son survives, and though we are still grieved that he has one from us in the body, we are not now tormented by the lack despair we knew before we received the comfort that apparently only Spiritualism can afford the bereaved.

"At a meeting my wife was asked by a lady what we thought of Spiritualists.

"We have found them the most kindly people. They know and understand with a depth of feeling that we have not found in the more orthodox."

Two or three weeks later there was another interesting sequel - a climax to the story - when the "Mystery Man," in a further article describing his sitting at Manchester with Mrs. Bullock, who, among other gifts, is a transfiguration medium, revealed his identity as that of Mr. Dan Bradbury, of Aldersyde, Broomgrove Road, Sheffield.

"Psychic News," prefacing this article, stated: "In Leeds, where he began his inquiry into Spiritualism, they called him the 'Mystery Man' because of the elaborate precautions this Yorkshire business man took to conceal his identity."

"Now," he says, "I have no objection to my name being used as the reason for my anonymity has disappeared - the mediums having given my name themselves."

Referring to the sitting with Mrs. Bullock, Mr. Bradbury commented, "We went into that seance room entire strangers to everybody, and yet we got a message through the medium immediately convincing and arresting."

The rest of his narrative is concerned with the remarkable evidence which Mrs. Bullock gave him and his wife, both at the seance and afterwards, but which it is unnecessary to reproduce here. It is sufficient to add that the proof they received amply confirmed the amazing evidence of their son's identity first given by Helen Hughes.

The next two records in this chapter both relate to parents whose lives were overshadowed by tragedy because of the death of their daughters, but who were translated from black despair to the incomparable consolation of certainty through the mediumship of Helen Hughes.

It was a "Psychic News" poster that changed the lives of Mr. and Mrs. Norman C. Sinclair, of 16, Princes Avenue, Seaburn, Sunderland, and set them on the road to the knowledge which is the only real anodyne for grief.

They owned a small yacht, which was moored near Boroughbridge, where this small, happy family of husband, wife and thirteen-year-old daughter spent their week-end.

"Suddenly tragedy, dark, stark tragedy, struck and left my wife and me nearly insane with grief;" wrote the husband. "Our child, Norma, was walking to the boat from Boroughbridge one Saturday evening when she was knocked down by a lorry and received injuries which proved fatal."

This was a terrible blow to the parents. "Away went our dreams of a happy, homely future," continued Mr.

Sinclair's narrative. "Away went joy and laughter and in its place... what? Fretting and heartaches, tears and black despair. My mind was filled with ghastly, loathsome, horrible thoughts, too terrible to tell."

The parents were still in this mental state, thinking the world "a vile place, convinced it was all rot about there being a loving Heavenly Father" when, driving through a Sunderland street, they saw a "Psychic News" placard, "Life After Death Proved."

Mrs. Sinclair went into the shop and bought a copy, which they hastened home to read. "Thank God for that paper!" wrote Mr. Sinclair. It brought them in touch with Spiritualism. They obtained psychic books and read of the proofs of Survival others had received.

Then a Spiritualist introduced them to Helen Hughes. Mr. Sinclair went to his first seance, a stranger to the medium except that she knew his name. Mrs. Hughes told him she could see a tall girl standing by his side. Norma was tall for her age.

He asked the medium what this girl was doing there, and she replied: "She has put both her arms round your neck, claiming you with love. She tells me you are her daddy." This was evidential, as Norma had always called him daddy, not father.

"She has her brother with her," continued the medium, and Mr. Sinclair's heart sank at this apparent misstatement, for Norma was their only child. "That is absolutely impossible," he declared, "I never had a son."

Helen Hughes, however, was quite undeterred by this objection, and persisted: "My guide has just told me that it is indeed your own son. He never knew life on earth. Your wife had a miscarriage years ago *(Even children unborn on earth are "born" on the Other Side).* In the spirit world he has been named John after your Uncle John, who has also passed on."

This amazed the father, who had completely forgotten, until then, that his wife had a miscarriage is years previously. It was also true that his Uncle John had passed on.

There were many subsequent sittings, but though he repeatedly asked the medium's guide (White Feather) to give him Norma's full name, the request was not acceded to. He was told that his daughter would give it herself one day.

The parents had practically given up hope of getting their daughter's full name when, a year later, the medium's second guide (Mazeeta), speaking through her, laughingly said, "Daddy Sinclair, you are going to get a surprise.

Mazeeta asked for pencil and paper. Mr. Sinclair gave her a pencil, but could find only the hack of an envelope on which she could write. "Oh, dear, this is too little, exclaimed Mazeeta, after one attempt, and added; laughing again, "Daddy Sinclair, your daddy is here and he says I have to write on the wall as there is plenty of room there."

This séance was held in complete darkness. When it was over and the light switched on, Mr. Sinclair examined the back of the envelope. On it was written in block letters "Norms Doreen." On the wall, he saw written "Norma Doreen Couly." The girl's christian names were Norma Doreen Coulson. - He considered the Couly very evidential, as he frequently nicknamed her "Couly,' a fact unknown to anybody else except his wife.

Remarkably enough, although printed in the dark, none of the block letters overlapped, either on the envelope or on the wall.

"Spiritualism has given us a new life," wrote Mr. Sinclair. The black, horrible thoughts have gone. Though we still yearn for our loved one, it is a wonderful comfort to know there is no death and that one day we will all meet again - a happy family."

Mr. Norman Dickson, of Windsor Avenue, Gateshead, Co. Durham, wrote the following account of how he and his wife were also convinced of the survival of their daughter through the mediumship of Helen Hughes:

"With the sole object of bringing some consolation to any who mourn the loss of a loved one, I proffer this contribution.

"At the beginning of this war we lost our only child at the age of eighteen. It seemed that some guiding light had been flicked out, leaving us in eternal darkness." Sincere expressions of sympathy gave little comfort to a mother and father who mourned the loss of a dear one.

To many, death appears to be the end and, in a physical sense, this is beyond doubt. There is a finality about death which brings to many of us, especially with materialist minds, nothing but sheer despondency. The impossibility to replace the joy of the physical presence, no matter how and where we search, must be admitted, but I believe that some of that joy can be retrieved by proof of Survival.

"Prior to our loss the question of Survival did not, perhaps, seriously engage the thoughts of the writer, not that this is uncommon in our very material world. Orthodox religion, excluding a few of its adherents, has done little to demonstrate, at least publicly, proof of continued existence after death, leaving many of us wondering at times why we are here. In no circumstances are we brought face to face with this question more forcibly than in times of bitter bereavement."

"We had read of some remarkable happenings, purporting to prove survival, and to experience the same ourselves became our absorbing desire. Reading had brought us comfort of mind, but we still required personal experience. Thus was partially obtained at Spiritualist meetings, where we heard messages given from the Other Side, these being apparently accepted by the recipients.

"Descriptions of persons said to be known to us when here on earth were often received by my wife and myself, and though some of the descriptions corresponded fairly accurately with the likeness of our own daughter, a vital link was always missing, her name.

"It was in August, 1940, nearly twelve months after the passing of our darling daughter, that we visited a medium known to many - Helen Hughes. Prior to this visit we were absolute strangers. We held a seance which consisted of the medium, my wife and myself, and it should be stated here that the strictest secrecy was observed regarding our personal affairs. All that the medium knew was our surname and that we were bereaved.

"During the séance a spirit entity (White Feather) spoke through the medium and referred to our 'daughter's' passing. The importance we attached to this remark was the use of the word 'daughter,' when, in fact, the medium did not know who it was we had lost. Another spirit, Mazeeta, then spoke, and we were told that she had a girl with her.

"Addressing my wife, Mazeeta said, 'They're telling me that you have a photograph in your bag.' *My wife had a photograph in her bag of our daughter.*

"Continuing, the control asked for a pencil and paper. A pencil was produced, but there was no paper at hand, although it seemed to me that writing would be rather difficult in the dark. Mazeeta then began spelling out something symbolically, and, taking the pencil from my hand, commenced (through the medium) to write on the photograph. After the seance the light was switched on and the medium remarked, 'Shall we see what has been written?'"

To their amazement and intense joy, records Mr. Dickson, they found that their daughter's name had been written on the plain side of the photograph. Neither he nor his wife could distinguish which was the plain side in the dark.

"If this phenomenon fails to impress even the most sceptical," he wrote, "then what is the explanation to discount it? . . . "At this same sitting our daughter assured us she was happy, and a message was received from my dear mother, whose name was also given. Through the medium she addressed both my wife and myself by our christian names, both of which were unknown to the medium."

At another seance, their daughter correctly referred to two birthdays falling in April, and at a further sitting certain incidents in the home were also accurately described.

On one occasion the medium saw standing beside them their daughter in a grey coat. "Thus was the colour of the coat she wore just before her passing, and which is still in our possession," continued Mr. Dickson's narrative.

"Can we reasonably cast aside such phenomena with the casual remark, 'There's nothing in it'? One is also prompted to ask whether it is 'sinful,' 'wicked,' 'unnatural,' or even 'a sign of an unbalanced mind' that one should express a desire, nay, a craving, for personal contact with a dearly loved one, and believe in its practicability.

"Were I to answer these questions in the affirmative, would I not, indeed, be unnatural, which, in itself, might amount to being unbalanced? Is not such a desire simply an expression of continued love and affection?

"Never have I felt more 'in tune with the Infinite' than at my first seance at which we received our daughter's name. No sermon, no expressions of the most diligent biblical student, could supplant that simple experience or create so beautiful an atmosphere."

Were all these parents deluded, swayed by emotion, robbed of their reasoning powers, hypnotised into believing in a few insubstantial nothings? Or were they convinced by clear, concise and incontrovertible evidence? The reader can judge the truth for himself. Truth is traduced, and ultimately triumphs in every age. Yesterday, evolution was denounced as "an infamous doctrine," sponsored by "charlatans and dupes." Today it is the turn of Spiritualism.

HELEN HUGHES

S. T. F. Dinner 1965

CHAPTER X
STRIKING TESTIMONY

> When whelmed are altar, priest and creed,
> When all the faiths have passed,
> Perhaps, from darkening incense freed,
> God may emerge at last."
> W. Watson, "New Poems."

The remainder of my material resolves itself into a miscellany illustrating the variety of Helen Hughes's experience as a medium.

Although there are numerous Press reports, and although Mrs. Hughes has received countless verbal expressions of thanks, and hundreds of letters - some of them fervently grateful - few sitters have ever recorded their personal impressions. This is unfortunate, as such testimony is valuable.

I have salvaged three typewritten records by methodical and enterprising sitters. The longest, running to six foolscap pages, is an account of a private sitting with Mrs. Hughes at Glasgow on December 16, 1936, booked under the name of Mr. Burns. It is a verbatim account of a sitting, during which Mrs. Hughes went into deep trance, but it is too long, circumstantial and intimate to quote in full.

Briefly, it describes, with a wealth of evidential detail, the return to his father, through the medium, of a little boy, Alex Baird, who died in hospital. The sitting lasted thirty minutes, during which the boy "took control" twice, in addition to the guides Mazeeta and White Feather. "I am completely unable to give on paper the totally different characteristics of each person," declared the father.

The next statement consists of three quarto pages, written by Mr. John Blackburn, of 30, Holystone Avenue, Whitley Bay, Northumberland. It is a concise report, containing exceptionally striking and convincing details, of which the following and extracts:

"My first connection with Spiritualism was as follows. It was in May, 1937 (my wife died on December 27, 1936).

"Early one morning in May (5 a.m.) I was going about my bedroom when I heard loud tapping on a large photograph of my wife. I went to a Spiritualist church the following Sunday. The medium there said, 'A lady is here and she says you have not to get up so early in the morning.' She then gave a very good description of my wife.

"The following week I got in touch with a friend in London (a Mr. S_____) who had a large experience with the best mediums in England. He arranged my first sitting with Mrs. Hughes, which took place on June 9, 1937

"I did not know this lady or any of her connections and she certainly did not know me or any of my friends, or even the gentleman who arranged the sitting.

"Mrs. Hughes went into trance and was controlled by Mazeeta, who said: 'Your wife has come. She says she is Jean Anderson Blackburn,, Your wife is claiming your ring, and says she is pleased to see you are wearing it. (I might say here that I had not worn this ring for nearly a year before my wife passed over, as it was getting thin, but a few weeks after, I had it thickened and started to wear it again.) She says she saw you put the flowers on the top of her coffin when it was lowered into the grave. There were three colours. (This is correct; before I left for the cemetery I went into my greenhouse and selected some primulas. These were the flowers I placed in the grave.) She says, 'You did not put me down there, and the day I died must be looked upon in future as my birthday, as I only started to live from that day.'

"Mazeeta continued, 'You have some pictures in your pocket.' I placed them on the table. She examined each one and told me who the persons were (members of my family). She also told me which ones had been taken on holiday and which ones locally. Also there was a photo of my favourite dog (a Great Dane named Duke). When

Mazeeta saw this she became very excited and said, 'That is Duke.'"

Referring to his wife again, Mazeeta said, "She also says, 'We had forty-two years of real honeymoon.' (This was the length of time we were married.)

"My wife," the report continues, "then took control and said: 'Mr. S_____'s son is here. He says he was listening to you talking to his father last week. (I live 250 miles from London, but I paid his father a visit there on the previous Tuesday.) Will you let him know he has now met me? He has helped me a lot. Bella (my sister) has also helped me. She is a spirit nurse. You remember I was in coma before I died. You kissed me and touched my hands. (I did.) Tell John (my son) and Ella (his wife) that I want to speak to them, and Ina and Lilian' (my two daughters)."

Mr. Blackburn then describes how Mr. S_____'s son and his sister Bella next took control and spoke to him, and also White Feather, who told him many things about his wife's passing and other family matters which were all correct.

"It was wonderful how easily the names came through," he concludes. "There were no errors of any kind whatever." The third typewritten record - a story with an amazing sequel is by Mrs. Gracie Clark, of Cambuslang Road, Farm Cross, Rutherglen, who wrote as follows:

"I have never had a sitting with Mrs. Hughes, nor does she know me. The following message was given at a packed evening meeting in Holland Street Spiritualist Church, Glasgow:

"'A lady who passed out this morning *(This is probably the earliest return after death of any communicator through Helen Hughes. She records that one of her uncles returned thirty - six hours after death.)* is asking for Gracie Clark. She says you ordered a wreath for her from Shearer's. The Shearers are related to you. Tell them at home that although she had spent nearly five years in different sanatoria, T.B. was not the cause of her passing.'

"I gave the message to the family that night, and when the death certificate was given the following day, after a post-mortem examination, it showed that she had passed out with bronchial trouble and a strained heart, and there was no T.B.

"With regard to the Shearers being related, to my knowledge that was not correct. I asked my husband and he denied relationship. But I spoke to Miss Shearer' who said that the middle name of the Shearer family was Clark, and the grandfathers were brothers."

Another tribute to the accuracy of Helen Hughes's mediumship, and to the consolation it brought the sitter, also came from Rutherglen, in the form of a letter from Mrs. Agnes Reid, of Rosslyn Avenue.

Mrs. Reid wrote to thank Helen Hughes for enabling her to communicate with her son, Sgt. Joseph Reid, radio operator in an Armstrong Whitley bomber which crashed outside Dundee on October 21, 1941. When the engines failed, Joseph Reid continued signalling until the last minute. His final message was, "We are going down now, at a thousand feet, in a gliding position." He and three other members of the crew were killed - there was only one survivor.

"I am writing this letter," said Mrs. Reid, "to thank you for the great help and comfort I have received from you this week. God gave to you what he gave to Paul, the power to help and comfort mothers, and I am sure there are many like me today."

Mrs. Reid's son spoke to her at a private sitting, through Mrs. Hughes, under trance control, and gave evidence which completely convinced her.

In this letter, Mrs. Reid also claimed the following personal psychic experience since the death of her son.

"It came to me three months after," she wrote, "when one night 1 was taken out of my body to where he is now. Up and up I knew I was going until I came to a beautiful oak door. I said, 'I wonder who lives in here - no handle, no place to put a key.' I knocked, and who opened it but my own boy.

"I said, 'Oh, son, they sent me word from Kinloss to say that you were dead.' 'No, ma,' he said, 'they only tell you that.' He opened the door wide so that I might enter, and to me it was all so lovely. I saw the other boys too, all dressed alike. The place they were in put me in mind of the song I used to sing to wounded soldiers during the last war, 'I Dreamt that I Dwelt in Marble Halls.'

"I came away out of the beautiful home, my boy seeing me to the door. I said, 'When will I see you again, son? He did not speak, but just looked at me, and his eyes seemed to say, 'That is not for me to say, ma,' and there I left him. . . . I was so happy I wanted to let the whole world know, and since that day I have never shed any more tears. My dear friend, I thank you. I will put you in my prayers every night and ask God to keep you well and happy so that you can go on with your wonderful work for many years to come."

Helen Hughes seldom makes predictions, and only two or three are recorded in this book. There is no more dangerous or uncertain ground in the whole of Spiritualistic research than that of prediction, and the subject is too involved to be discussed here. One point, however, should be stressed. Many inquirers particularly of the type who believe that the chief function of palmists and clairvoyants generally is to "tell their future" on request labour under the delusion that the ability of mediums to forecast coming events is the primary test and the major mission of Spiritualism.

It is not. Prediction plays only a small part in the utterances of mediums. There is ample evidence for Survival, relating to the past and the present, without recourse to prophecy. Sceptics who base their judgment of Spiritualism solely on whether or not the future can be accurately predicted, or who reveal a disposition to demand "tips" for horse and dog races display a perfect blend of stupidity and cupidity.

Predictions are often astonishingly accurate, but they are by no means infallible, particular) with regard to dates. Those on the spirit planes can see farther than we can, but their forecasts are not *invariably* correct.

Helen Hughes is not an orator, and seldom makes long speeches. Her chief mission is to deliver messages evidencing Survival. Occasionally, however, she speaks on the philosophical side of Spiritualism, and answers problems at "question time." The following, to which she once replied, are of interest because they are so frequently asked at Spiritualist meetings:

"Is Spiritualism of God or the Devil?"

"Spiritualism heals broken hearts, gives warning of impending dangers,' gives advice with uncanny wisdom, comforts in bereavement, helps in the perplexities of daily life, restores people to health, and functions in countless other ways. If all this wonderful enlightenment were the work of the Devil, well, he is surely not as bad as he has been painted through the ages. But there can be only one answer - Spiritualism is a God."

"Do we disturb the dead?"

"Definitely no! How can we? They are not dead. The majority of people who have not yet fully studied the principles of Spiritualism are under the misapprehension that those who have passed away have gone to a place of rest and must not be disturbed. We cannot disturb the dead because there ore no dead. There is merely a change in the form of life. Life after death is just as active and progressive as before."

"Why don't Spiritualists fear death?"

"What is there to fear? Death means passing into a more beautiful, more peaceful world - a place where everyone has his heart's desire, where progress, peace and happiness prevail."

One of Helen Hughes's most likeable characteristics is her unfailing optimism and sense of humour. Like all intelligent Spiritualists, she realises that it is illogical to regard the afterlife with sanctimonious solemnity. She believes in the essential cheerfulness of the subject.

Spiritualism is gradually untangling that dismal confusion of mournfulness with reverence. I sometimes smile when I hear the orthodox accusing Spiritualism of being "morbid, eerie, uncanny, unbalancing, depressing," and so forth. To me there is nothing so depressing and intellectually uninspiring as the unmitigated misery of the average church service. Compare the pious platitudes, outworn creeds and dreary dirges and dogmas of effete Orthodoxy with the interesting and inspiring evidence of the seance or Spiritualist meeting. Surely dolefulness is not divine and laughter has its place in the scheme of things.

It is the orthodox who make religion morbid. Spiritualists could turn their "vale of tears" into a valley of advancement, and sweep away the unoriginal stupidity of their "original sin." They often wonder to what the orthodox imagine they are being "reverent" in regarding the dead as lying in the grave until the day of doom. Spiritualists do not merely believe, they know that life goes on, that communication is a fact, and that it is as cheerful and natural to talk to the dead - though unfortunately not so easily accomplished - as to talk to a friend on the telephone.

Helen Hughes is sincerely sympathetic when speaking to the bereaved about their loved ones, but she is never maudlin. Though by no means flippant or facetious, she is not afraid to make a joke if the occasion arises. Quite frequently the spirit communicators themselves "crack a joke" - often a family one which is immediately recognised - and which, therefore, is in itself evidential.

I remember Helen Hughes pointing to a member of the audience at a meeting in the Usher Hall, Edinburgh, in May, 1944, and asking, on behalf of the spirit to whose voice she was listening, "Did somebody pull your leg before the meeting when you spoke about 'coming to the spooks'?" The recipient agreed, amid hearty laughter, that this was quite correct.

I have noted one or two passages, in cuttings and books, bearing on the subject of humour, which Helen Hughes has marked, and which I think afford an insight into her character. Here they are:

"Spiritualism will always be popular because it is full of the means of stimulating Joy. To know that those who have passed away are in a happier state than ours, and that their life is normal and healthy, is a splendid stimulation to happiness."

"The idea that a departed friend ought to be occupied wholly and entirely with grave matters, and ought not to remember jokes and fun, is a gratuitous claim which has to be abandoned. Humour does not cease with earth life. Why should it?"

One of the most interesting speculations ever made regarding the future of Spiritualism was that of the possibility of constructing some super - sensitive electrical device - perhaps a development of the wireless receiver - by means of which direct communication could be established with the spirit world.

Sir Ernest Fisk, chairman of Amalgamated Wireless (Australasia) Ltd., and managing director of Electrical and Musical Industries Ltd., who is a radio pioneer, and one of the most prominent personalities in the wireless world, declared early in 1944 that evidence was accumulating, as a result of the work ,of scientists, that the spirits of the dead inhabited the ionised ether beyond the earth's atmosphere, and suggested that scientists might one day be able to develop mechanical means whereby the dead and the living can communicate.

As an analogy to his theory, he pointed out that in radio-location the limits of the physical world were transcended often unexpectedly, he was reported to have "shocked ordered opinion." In an interview with "Truth," an Australian newspaper, he said: "When I say that the dead are alive, I cannot prove it. Neither, however, can people prove that there is no life after death. Communication, if it could be established by radio science, would afford that proof."

The invention of such an apparatus would be revolutionary in its results. It would prove Survival beyond dispute. By superseding the medium, it would rule out the objection of sceptics that the "human element" and the subconscious are responsible for all types of psychic phenomena. Spiritualists might object that "mechanisation" of contact between the two worlds is undesirable, but it is safe to assert that whatever *can* be done *will* be done. If science can demonstrate this tremendous truth, it will render an inestimable service to mankind, and Spiritualism will be vindicated. The means by which great ends are brought about often appear prosaic, but the end ennobles the means.

At a meeting in Edinburgh Psychic College in January, 1945, when Helen Hughes was controlled by White Feather, who invited questions from the audience, I asked whether such a device was ever likely to be invented.

"Not in this generation," he replied. "There will be the apparatus. We are making the preparations. It is not impossible. If you could only see the organisation here for the same purpose of breaking through, and finding the way for easier communication! The day is coming when you yourself will witness the very thing you are asking. You will 'listen-in.' The world today calls it direct voice, and it will come."

If White Feather is correct in his forecast that the apparatus will not be devised in thin generation, it rather seems as though I shall have to "listen-in" from the Other Side. I look forward to hearing what the sceptics say. At least they could not prosecute an electrical apparatus under the Vagrancy Act or the Witchcraft Act!

Helen Hughes travelled under all kinds of conditions to fulfil her wartime engagements. Sometimes she stood for hour in crowded trains, or sat on her suitcase in the corridor. Eventually the strain began to tell on her frail constitution, but she struggled to continue her work until, in the middle of January, 1945, she was obliged to take a long rest.

Her last meeting before this break was at the Edinburgh Psychic College, where she has so many friends. She was suffering from an uncontrollable cough, with acute throat irritation, but, reluctant to disappoint her audience, she pluckily attempted to complete her demonstration. After delivering several messages, she was seized with a violent paroxysm of coughing. She sat down, her head bowed forward, and in a moment White Feather had taken control.

The coughing immediately ceased, and for about ten minutes the guide, speaking in tones which one spectator described as being "as clear as a bell," continued to give messages to the audience.

Not once during this period was there the slightest suggestion of coughing. The guide - explaining that he was using another part of the throat - spoke continuously in a firm and confident voice. He said that Mrs. Hughes's cold was so severe that he had decided to work for her that evening.

The climax came when the guide relinquished control. Instantaneously, Mrs. Hughes was again convulsed with coughing, and the meeting ended.

Other meetings at which she was to have demonstrated were abandoned. Mrs. Hughes afterwards intimated that her doctors had advised her that unless she stopped work for three months she might develop chronic laryngitis.

This was not the first incident of its kind in her experience. At the International Spiritualist Congress, Glasgow, 1937, Mrs. Hughes, replying to questions regarding her sensations and reactions in trance, recalled a similar occurrence.

In reply to the question, "Are mediums in trance disturbed by noise, etc.?" she said that once she was suffering from whooping cough, which kept her and the household awake. At last her condition was such that her guide announced that she must have rest, and that they would put her into trance and stop her coughing for four hours.

White Feather told Mr. Hughes that he could talk to him if he wished, and they conversed for over two hours. Then the guide said that Mrs. Hughes had become "so unruly and so anxious to return" that they had to allow her to do so. But the cough did not return until the four hours had elapsed.

With regard to this rather interesting point, that the medium had become "unruly," it should be noted that she has no recollection of these trance episodes. In deep trance the spirit is detached from the body except for the psychic or "silver cord," and, according to available information on the subject, is able to converse with those on the Other Side.

I once heard Mazeeta say, when Helen Hughes was about to emerge from trance at the Edinburgh College, that the medium was "running back" - apparently a parallel case.

"Maxwell Scot?" wrote of the way in which she uses her voice as follows:

"In her normal voice Mrs. Hughes speaks with a pleasant enough light soprano, but she continually uses the upper register. She has had lessons in elocution, but has evidently not been taught to breathe correctly or to use the lower register. In her public work she makes that common mistake among women speakers of raising her voice still higher when she wishes to emphasise a point. She strains her voice unnecessarily.

"But when White Feather spoke, all these characteristics disappeared. The voice was deep, resonant, austere. It was the voice of an orator - which Mrs. Hughes is not. I doubt very much whether she could talk like that if she tried for years."

The family moved about ten years ago to their present home, in Dalton-le-Dale, near Sunderland, once described as "nestling in a rustic dale in the midst of the Durham coalfields."

This home is to Helen Hughes as much a headquarters or base of operations as a dwelling-place. She is domesticated, and fond of her home, but the demands upon her time are pressing, and she makes it her duty to meet them as far as humanly possible.

Even when at home, after her long journeys, she cannot completely relax. At times she has a heavy postbag - she has had letters from India, Australia, the U.S.A., Canada, Africa, Norway and Sweden, and many other parts of the world and there are frequent telegrams and telephone calls.

The story of her life would not be complete without a brief tribute to her husband, who has always recognised her value to the world at large, and encouraged her in her great work, despite the many breaks it occasions in their home life. Incidentally, he retired from his work in the mines about seventeen years ago to enter the building trade. He and Mrs. Hughes have led an exceptionally happy married life. Mr. Hughes resembles his wife in character in many ways - he is quiet, amiable and unassuming, a home-lover, and a man of simple tastes.

If anyone had asked the Ministry of Labour during the war whether Helen Hughes was engaged on "work of national importance," they might have received a negative reply. Nevertheless, at least in the opinion of Spiritualists, she was performing the most valuable and humanitarian work of all the consolation of the bereaved - and her many journeys really were necessary. From one corner of the land to the other, all through the war, she carried the torch of the new knowledge, and wherever she went she was acclaimed as a living worker of miracles.

I hope that, when her life story comes to be amplified, not only will the bounds of Spiritualism itself have been immeasurably widened, but that there will be many more chapters of travels and triumphs to record.

THE END

SDU PUBLICATIONS
PIONEER SERIES

J. J. MORSE
Practical Occultism and A Spirit Interviewed

J.J. Morse is regarded as one of Spiritualism's finest trance mediums. This volume brings together for the first time two books about him, his mediumship and the 'Spirit Control' known as Tien Sien Tie.

NETTIE COLBURN MAYNARD
Was Abraham Lincoln A Spiritualist?

At the height of the American civil war Nettie Coburn, then only a young woman, gave trance sittings to the American President. What did the Spirit world tell him?

She kept it a secret for over 30 years, only committing it to paper at the end of her life.

This is the story of one of Spiritualism's finest trance mediums and what the Spirit world told the President in a time of crisis.

ESTELLE ROBERTS
Fifty Years A Medium

I once heard Gordon Higginson describe Estelle Roberts as "the perfect medium". This book is her autobiography.

Minister Steven Upton
01909 489828
steven@s-upton.com